THE
BEST GIFTS

THE BEST GIFTS

Seeking Earnestly for Spiritual Power

ZACHARY M. HUTCHINS

Covenant Communications, Inc.

Cover image: *Interrupting Angels* © Annie Henrie Nader. For more information visit www.anniehenrie.com.

Cover design by Christina Marcano © 2019 by Covenant Communications, Inc.

Published by Covenant Communications, Inc.
American Fork, Utah

Copyright © 2019 by Zachary M. Hutchins
All rights reserved. No part of this book may be reproduced in any format or in any medium without the written permission of the publisher, Covenant Communications, Inc., P.O. Box 416, American Fork, UT 84003. This work is not an official publication of The Church of Jesus Christ of Latter-day Saints. The views expressed within this work are the sole responsibility of the author and do not necessarily reflect the position of The Church of Jesus Christ of Latter-day Saints, Covenant Communications, Inc., or any other entity.

Printed in the United States of America
First Printing: October 2019

26 25 24 23 22 21 20 19   10 9 8 7 6 5 4 3 2 1

ISBN: 978-1-52441-084-1

For Gabriel, David, Kenneth, Ruth, Lincoln, Alara, Rockwell, and—I hope—Priscilla.

TABLE OF CONTENTS

Acknowledgments..ix

Foreword by Whitney Johnson..xi

Part One: Spiritual Gifts in These Days...1

    Chapter 1: Always Remember..7

    Chapter 2: For What They Are Given...19

    Chapter 3: Have Miracles Ceased?..33

    Chapter 4: Deny Not the Gifts of God..47

Part Two: Case Studies from the Book of Mormon..63

    Chapter 5: Lehi and the Gift of Gratitude..69

    Chapter 6: Abish and the Gift of Gathering...83

    Chapter 7: Teancum and the Gift of Being Anxiously Engaged............97

    Chapter 8: Nephi, Son of Helaman, and the Gift of Unwearyingness..109

Afterword: A More Excellent Way..121

ACKNOWLEDGMENTS

I FIRST CONCEIVED OF THIS book more than fifteen years ago, in a dorm room at the Centro de Treinamento Missionário of São Paulo, Brasil, where I was inspired by my associations with the other members of District 38-D. They endured weeks of interrupted sleep, as my alarm went off well before 6:30 a.m. so that I could learn more about spiritual gifts, and as we sought for the gift of tongues together, we truly became one. My first debt, then, is to Sisters Galloway, Bourne, Lowe, and McDonald and to Elders Hansen, Bradshaw, Winn, Fleming, and Porter. A similar expression of gratitude is owed to each of my two dozen companions in the Missão Brasil João Pessoa, who exercised patience as I sought for other gifts, especially the gifts of humility and charity. All too often I failed and came to appreciate the spiritual gifts that they brought into our companionship only after our time together had ended. I am particularly grateful for the companionship and conversation offered by my trainer, Elder Baker, who talked through many of the ideas in this book with me long before they took shape in written form.

Although the friends who offered words of encouragement along the way are too numerous to name, three deserve special mention. Mike Arbon was the first person who ever asked me to do research on a religious topic; that invitation opened my eyes to a new world of possibility and awakened a hunger for knowledge that has yet to be sated. His expressions of respect and friendship to a young man still finding his way in the world meant everything. Akram Khater, more than anyone else, helped me to recognize the value of good questions as a gateway to learning. Although I stood at the front of the classroom where we met, he taught me far more than I taught him. Perhaps the most valuable lesson he shared, by both precept and example, is that truth must be sought fearlessly and courageously, without regard for the consequences of that search. And Kylan Rice is the reason I began to write, at long last. He has always believed in me far more than I deserve, and his belief fairly willed this book into being. There will always be a place for him and his at our table.

Once I finally began to write, family members offered invaluable support. My parents have always been my biggest cheerleaders, and siblings encouraged me from a distance. But it was Alana, my wonderful wife, who helped me to make space and time for this endeavor, adjusting her own sleep schedule—like my CTM companions so many years ago—so that I could steal a few minutes each morning to write before our children awoke. Those wonderful, overwhelming, noisy, precious children have always been my intended audience. I hope that each of them will read this book someday and come to a closer relationship with the Giver of all good gifts.

Although most of what is worthwhile in this book could ultimately be traced back to others, the mistakes or misapprehensions which remain are mine and mine alone. I have been grateful for the aid of Ashley Gebert, my wonderfully generous editor at Covenant, in preparing this manuscript, but only the great Editor above could be expected to correct *all* of my errata. When I, like Benjamin Franklin, am granted a celestial second edition, I expect that He will do so—and I look forward to those loving reproofs.

FOREWORD
BY WHITNEY JOHNSON

I've known Ann (that's what I'll call her) professionally for about ten years. Not well, but there is collegiality and a feeling of affection. Some months ago, she reached out after her firstborn child, a seemingly happy twenty-something young man with a lot to live for, had suddenly taken his life. Ann was heartbroken and questioning her long and dearly held faith. My brother took his own life several years ago, and I hoped that I could provide some perspective that would offer comfort. I did my best, praying in my heart for inspiration, as Ann and I spoke. And then we parted.

During my morning exercise routine not long ago, I had this thought: email Ann. I hadn't thought of our conversation for months. Like a roadrunner, the impression darted in and out of my mind so quickly that I almost missed it. But I wrote it down, and when I finished exercising, I emailed her a brief note—*I am thinking of you, sending my love.* Within hours, she wrote back saying, "Tomorrow is the first anniversary of my son's death." It was clear to me I had received a prompting. I hope that because I acted on it, Ann's burden was lighter, even if only for a moment.

In one of his first general conference addresses as prophet, President Nelson encouraged us to "Write the thoughts that come to your mind. Record your feelings and follow through with actions that you are prompted to take. As you repeat this process day after day, month after month, year after year, you will 'grow into the principle of revelation.' . . . Stretch beyond your current spiritual ability to receive personal revelation."[1] Having listened to this conference talk many times, I know that my experience with Ann, the prompting I received, was an opportunity for me to grow in the principle of revelation. After reading Zach Hutchins's mind- and heart-expanding book, *The Best Gifts*, I also better understand that this is a spiritual gift.

1 Russell M. Nelson, "Revelation for the Church, Revelation for Our Lives," *Ensign* or *Liahona*, May 2018.

In my professional life, I've developed a framework for personal disruption, a mechanism by which teams and organizations reach their collective potential. One of the seven components of this framework is playing to our distinctive strengths—bringing to the team something we do well that others do not. Frequently, people have little sense of what their distinctive strengths are. The things we do best can be so natural, so reflexive that—like breathing—they are invisible to us. Or even if we do recognize our greatest strengths, their ease may lead us to underestimate their value.

Having read Zach's book, I now wonder whenever we are able to do something so well that we don't even notice we do it, or attach any value to it—like offering a smile or a friendly word of encouragement—if these intrinsic abilities are spiritual gifts. I wonder if we live in a day where it seems that miracles have ceased, that they have passed, simply because we don't attach much value to being nice and easy to get along with (at least we don't tend to compensate people for it!), and in a similar way, we don't value the majority of spiritual gifts. These gifts abound but aren't flashy; many of us just don't recognize them for what they are. What I love about the gospel of Jesus Christ is that we don't have to wonder about our gift(s). When we receive a patriarchal blessing, we typically learn about at least one of them. A starting point. As we pay attention to the simple things we do that make a difference for good, we will discover others.

Zach writes that the development of gifts is a team sport. I love the story of entrepreneur and philanthropist Dianna Newton Anderson. Her college basketball coach had them shoot from everywhere on the court and memorize their percentages—not unusual. But he also had them memorize everyone else's percentages too, so they could literally play to their strengths. What are the strengths or the gifts of people around you? It's been said that *the cobbler's children have no shoes*. Typically we interpret this to mean that we don't attend to those closest to us, but I think we can attach a different meaning. To me it means that we can't use our strengths, or in this case, our spiritual gifts, to bless ourselves. And this is good; it means we need each other. In the giving of our gifts, the playing to our strengths with each other, we become bound, our hearts knit together. Sealed.

We might also be surprised by where we find these gifts, to discover that members of The Church of Jesus Christ don't have a corner on this market. To everyone is a gift given. Everyone. While on a recent business trip to Sydney, Australia, I interacted with a bellman several times. He was a petite, older man from Chile named Raul. We didn't speak for more than a minute or two at a time. But there was something very special about him. As I checked out of the hotel, I told him so. *There is something about you. Something about you deeply good and kind. I can feel it.* I had experienced a spiritual gift—Raul's spiritual gift of kindness.

As you read *The Best Gifts*, you will better understand what spiritual gifts are and, specifically, what yours are. You'll be reminded that the best way to "earnestly seek" after these gifts is in the service of others. By exercising our gifts, we can disrupt who we are and start to become the person God wants us to be. When we have eyes to see, there is evidence of spiritual gifts everywhere—miracles have not ceased.

One of my favorite quotes is Ralph Waldo Emerson's: "Rings and other jewels are not gifts, but apologies for gifts. The only gift is a portion of thyself." Through Zach Hutchins's book, I've heard it again for the first time.

To each of us is given a gift
By the Giver of Gifts.
Give even a portion of yourself, there will be more.
He's just waiting for you to ask.

PART ONE

Spiritual Gifts in These Days

When Joseph Smith spoke to others of his first vision, in which he saw the embodied forms of God the Father and His Only Begotten Son and heard each of them speak, local ministers rejected this account of divine visitation. The boy related his experience to a Methodist preacher, but the clergyman responded "with great contempt, saying it was all of the devil, that there were no such things as visions or revelations in these days" (JS—H 1:21). Thus, from the very beginning of Joseph's labors as a prophet, and even before the official organization of The Church of Jesus Christ of Latter-day Saints some ten years later, many of the key theological questions confronting him and his followers concerned the nature and availability of spiritual gifts. Had such things "ceased with the apostles," as the Methodist preacher alleged (JS—H 1:21)? If not, who was eligible to receive these divine manifestations? How could one distinguish between the power of God and that of Satan? These and similar questions led Joseph to inquire of the Lord, generating many of his earliest recorded revelations. A belief in and understanding of spiritual gifts was fundamental to the work of the Restoration and remains an important but under-examined tenet of Latter-day Saint theology.

Perhaps because Joseph's first revelatory experience prompted skepticism and doubt from individuals who believed that spiritual gifts had ceased with the Apostles, his second communication from heaven included an unequivocal declaration that these gifts continue to be available to the children of men in modern times. The ancient prophet Moroni appeared to Joseph three times on the evening of September 21, 1823, and each time he quoted the words of Joel: "I will pour out my spirit upon all flesh; and your sons and your daughters shall prophesy, your old men shall dream dreams, your young men shall see visions: and also upon the servants and upon the handmaids in those days will I pour out my spirit" (Joel 2:28–29). Moroni explained to Joseph that this long-foretold outpouring of spiritual gifts "was not yet fulfilled, but was soon to be" (JS—H 1:41). Central to the work of the Restoration with which Moroni charged the boy prophet was a belief in spiritual gifts and a recognition of their role in bringing to pass the salvation and unification of the human family. Indeed, Moroni's explanation identified this dispensation and these days as a time when spiritual gifts would be made manifest in greater abundance than ever before. Although we still speak of and seek after spiritual gifts today, almost two hundred years since Moroni's appearance to Joseph, these aptitudes cultivated in the premortal realm and administered through the merits and mercies of Jesus Christ rarely receive the sustained attention offered to other topics that are central to our faith.

Accordingly, this book begins with an examination of the Savior's commandment that we are to remember and seek after spiritual gifts always (see D&C 46:8–10). Chapter one considers the links between this theological imperative and our love of Jesus Christ, offering practical counsel on how best to honor such a lofty standard. Because if we "do keep his commandments he doth bless [us] and prosper [us]," our efforts to remember and to seek after spiritual gifts draw down the blessings of heaven immediately (Mosiah 2:22, 24). Chapter two investigates the purpose or reason for which spiritual gifts are bestowed, emphasizing the blessings of unity and love that these gifts cultivate within and between members of the body of Christ. The unanimity and collective charity that come with the exercise of spiritual gifts were dramatically and publicly manifest on the day of Pentecost and, centuries later, during the Kirtland Temple dedication, but these exceptional outpourings of gifts are just that: exceptional. Chapter three asks why we rarely, if ever, see similarly dramatic and public demonstrations of spiritual gifts in our own day, taking the experience of Mormon and Moroni—who lived when "there were no gifts"—as a point of comparison (Mormon 1:14). These two ancient prophets saw our day in vision, writing to modern readers of the Book of Mormon that "Jesus Christ hath shown you unto me" (Mormon 8:35). Knowing that many in our time would side with the Methodist minister who chastised Joseph and declare that the day of miracles has ceased, Mormon testified that miracles and spiritual gifts will continue "so long as time shall last, or the earth shall stand, or there shall be one man upon the face thereof to be saved" (Moroni 7:36). Chapter four affirms that miracles and spiritual gifts are manifest in modern times; it identifies numerous modern examples of gifts exercised in public and offers counsel on how to recognize these gifts as manifestations of divine power.

The first four chapters provide a primer on key principles, declared in scripture, that govern the development, use, and recognition of spiritual gifts. Those principles are broadly applicable to individuals in a wide variety of ecclesiastical or cultural contexts as they seek to develop any one of the numerous gifts offered by God to His children. Their importance to our spiritual welfare in this dispensation is suggested by the emphasis with which Moroni, the messenger of the Restoration, spoke and wrote of spiritual gifts.

In addition to his teachings on the night of his first visit with Joseph Smith, Moroni also taught about spiritual gifts in his personal contributions to the Book of Mormon. His writings emphasize the core doctrine and basic ordinances of the gospel; they provide direction on the most important elements of Church membership and worship. He gives the language for the sacramental prayers and details the procedures for priesthood ordination and the conferral of the Holy Ghost. He describes the administration of Church meetings and stipulates that each member of the Church must be numbered, remembered, and nourished. To these most basic, fundamental ordinances and principles, Moroni appends the doctrine of spiritual gifts. With his last words, the prophet entrusted with the final abridgment, safekeeping, and delivery of the Book of Mormon prioritized the seeking of spiritual gifts as a directive for our day. Our desire to obtain spiritual gifts and our emphasis on their development should, accordingly, be comparable to the attention and effort we devote to other core doctrines of the gospel. We should remember them always and seek after them with the same consistent focus that we give to our next ordinance on the covenant pathway and with the same yearning attention we give to spiritual milestones such as baptism, priesthood ordination, and the sacrament.

During his apostolic ministry, President Dallin H. Oaks lamented, "We know too little about spiritual gifts."[1] But a knowledge of our Heavenly Father's "best gifts" is freely available to all who seek earnestly for that blessing, and President Russell M. Nelson has pleaded with Church members to make their development and use a priority (D&C 46:8). "I urge you," he said, "with all the hope of my heart, to pray to understand *your spiritual gifts*—to cultivate, use, and expand them, even more than you ever have. You will change the world as you do so."[2] This prophetic charge should motivate each of us to repent—to do better and be better in preparing ourselves for the sacred work

---

1 Dallin H. Oaks, "Spiritual Gifts" [Brigham Young University devotional, Mar. 1, 1986], speeches.byu.edu.

2 Russell M. Nelson, "Sisters' Participation in the Gathering of Israel," *Ensign* or *Liahona*, November 2018.

with which the Savior and His prophet have entrusted us by learning more about spiritual gifts and exercising them more regularly in His service.

CHAPTER 1
ALWAYS REMEMBER

When we as members of The Church of Jesus Christ of Latter-day Saints take the emblems of the sacrament each week, we renew our baptismal covenants, promising to "bear one another's burdens . . . mourn with those that mourn . . . comfort those that stand in need of comfort, and to stand as witnesses of God at all times and in all things" (Mosiah 18:8–9). The words of the prayers offered by priesthood holders each week on this occasion, sanctifying bread and water to the souls of those who will eat and drink, were established by revelation. Those prayers stipulate that participants should "always remember" Jesus Christ (D&C 20:77, 79). Few commandments are more difficult to keep; however, always remembering the Savior is the only way we can fulfill our covenantal responsibility to witness of Jesus Christ morning, noon, and night, whether at work, "at home, at school, at play."[1]

We struggle to always remember our Redeemer because, as a condition of mortality, each of us is subject to what Nephi calls "the weakness which is in [us], according to the flesh" (1 Nephi 19:6). One aspect of that weakness is the natural tendency for our minds to wander: it is challenging, even on our best days and in the most favorable circumstances, for the human brain to remain focused on a single thought for an extended period of time. Social science research has demonstrated again and again that purposeful, intensive thought is difficult to sustain; a portion of the brain is constantly scanning the surrounding environment for new stimuli, and resisting the urge to let our minds wander is tiring. As the Nobel-winning psychologist Daniel Kahneman writes, "the idea of mental energy is more than a mere metaphor. . . . And effortful mental activity appears to be especially expensive in the currency of glucose."[2] We are, as mortal beings of flesh and blood, easily distracted and

---

[1] "Jesus Wants Me for a Sunbeam," *Children's Songbook*, 60.
[2] Daniel Kahneman, *Thinking, Fast and Slow* (New York: Farrar, Straus and Giroux, 2011), 43.

in possession of finite, exhaustible resources; to consciously always remember something—anything—is a tremendously difficult task.

The experience of the Apostle Peter illustrates this challenge nicely. After the Savior fed the five thousand, He sent His disciples across the sea while He remained on shore alone to pray. That night, as the Apostles toiled, rowing their way across the water, Jesus appeared, "walking on the sea." Peter called to his Master, "Lord, if it be thou, bid me come unto thee on the water." And Jesus said, "Come." Courageously, Peter stepped out of the boat and, in a miraculous demonstration of faith, "walked on the water, to go to Jesus" (Matthew 14:25–29). In that particular moment, Peter was wholly focused on the Savior; his eye, in scriptural parlance, was single (see Matthew 6:22). But even when his very life depended on maintaining that focus, Peter's eye and then his mind wandered. After rowing all night, he must have been both tired and hungry. Then, when he "saw the wind boisterous, he was afraid," and in that moment of weakness, as his eyes and attention drifted from the Savior, he began to sink (Matthew 14:30). If always thinking of Jesus was a challenge for Peter, the Lord's chief Apostle, who could see the Master in front of him and whose survival depended on that focus, it will also be a challenge for us.

Because it is so hard for us as mortals to do anything "always," our Father in Heaven and His Son use that word rarely. In fact, the sacramental commandment to always remember Jesus Christ is echoed in only one other passage of scripture—in the forty-sixth section of the Doctrine and Covenants, where Jesus Christ declares, "I would that ye should always remember, and always retain in your minds what those gifts are, that are given unto the church." Church members are to "seek ye earnestly the best gifts, always remembering for what they are given" (D&C 46:10, 8). Three times in as many verses of scripture, the Savior uses the word *always* to describe how often we should consider the spiritual gifts He has made available to the Church and the purposes for which He has given them.

Rather than thinking of this commandment as establishing a second, competing priority for our mental energy, we might regard this directive to "always remember" as an extension of our sacramental covenant, whereby Jesus Christ directs our attention—our remembering—to particular aspects of His identity. When we promise to remember Jesus Christ during the sacramental prayer, there is no accompanying instruction as to whether we should remember His role as the Creator, as the only perfect man to walk the earth, or as the firstfruits of the Resurrection. We might consider His role as the "good shepherd

[who] giveth his life for [his] sheep" (John 10:11), the "Lamb slain from the foundation of the world" (Revelation 13:8), the "Bishop of your souls" (1 Peter 2:25), or "The Prince of Peace" (Isaiah 9:6), among many others. By instructing the members of His Church to always remember the nature and purposes of the gifts described in section 46 of the Doctrine and Covenants, Jesus Christ calls our attention to His identity as a giver of gifts—gifts enabling those who keep covenant with Him to thrive amid the challenges of mortality.[3] Those gifts are an extension of himself; as Ralph Waldo Emerson once declared, "Rings and other jewels are not gifts, but apologies for gifts. The only gift is a portion of thyself. . . . A man's biography is conveyed in his gift."[4] Thus, to remember the spiritual gifts made available to us is also, necessarily, to remember the Giver and His life.

Scripture is replete with examples of Jesus Christ endowing His covenant people with gifts. Before Adam and Eve left the Garden of Eden, Jesus Christ, in His role as Jehovah, God of the Old Testament, gave them "coats of skins" that would offer them protection from the inclement conditions of a fallen world (Moses 4:27). When it came time for Adam to make a record of his interactions with God, he wrote a "book of remembrance . . . for it was given unto as many as called upon God to write by the spirit of inspiration" (Moses 6:5). Written language itself seems to have been a gift, meant to facilitate intergenerational learning; Adam's descendants would clarify that this book of remembrance was composed "according to the pattern given by the finger of God" (Moses 6:46).[5] Later, when Abraham made covenant with Jehovah, the Messiah introduced himself as a giver of gifts: "I am the Lord that brought thee out of Ur of the Chaldees, to give thee this land to inherit it" (Genesis 15:7). Abraham was also given, on that occasion, a promise of posterity and priesthood (see Abraham 2:9–11). Jehovah's gifts to His covenant-keeping people are so numerous that He promises to "open you the windows of heaven, and pour you out a blessing, that there shall not be room enough to receive it" (Malachi 3:10). He is both the Giver and the Gift received "without money and without price" (Isaiah 55:1).

The spiritual gifts that we are commanded to remember in the Doctrine and Covenants are made available through the merits, mercy, and power of Jesus Christ. Exhorting his future readers—you and I—to seek after spiritual gifts, Moroni writes that "all these gifts come by the Spirit of Christ" (Moroni

---

3 See also M. Russell Ballard, "Precious Gifts from God," *Ensign* or *Liahona*, May 2018.
4 Ralph Waldo Emerson, "Gifts," in *Works of Ralph Waldo Emerson* (London: George Routledge and Sons, 1897), 117.
5 See also Hugh W. Nibley, "Genesis of the Written Word," in *Nibley on the Timely and the Timeless: Classic Essays of Hugh W. Nibley*, 2nd ed. (Provo: Religious Studies Center, Brigham Young University, 2004), 111–41.

10:17). The "Spirit of Christ" is an unusual phrase that occurs only five times in scripture, and Moroni uses it here as a synonym for the Light of Christ. Moroni learned in an epistle from his father, Mormon, that "the Spirit of Christ is given to every man, that he may know good from evil; wherefore I show unto you the way to judge," and he further explains that "the light by which ye may judge . . . is the light of Christ" (Moroni 7:16, 18). Spiritual gifts come by the Light of Christ, and part of our covenantal obligation to "always remember" these gifts is a need to "remember that every good gift cometh of Christ" (Moroni 10:18).

The Light of Christ is that "true Light, which lighteth every man that cometh into the world" (John 1:9). All who are born into mortality are touched by its influence, whether or not they have entered into a covenant relationship with God. President Marion G. Romney taught that this Light of Christ is "the source of one's conscience," a guide prompting God's children to recognize truth and to act in harmony with His eternal laws.[6] Prophets have taught that the inventors, engineers, and scientists whose discoveries benefit the human race are often directed by the influence of the Light of Christ; so, too, are the composers, artists, and performers whose creations bring beauty into existence.[7] Freely given to all individuals, the Light of Christ inspires each man and woman who does not reject its influence.

Similarly, every member of the human family enters mortality as the possessor of at least one spiritual gift. There is a wide array of spiritual gifts made available to each of God's children, but "all have not every gift given unto them; for there are many gifts, and to every man is given a gift by the Spirit of God" (D&C 46:11). The Spirit or Light of Christ endows every individual with a conscience—an awareness of eternal laws—and it also provides every man, woman, and child with at least one spiritual gift. Scripture teaches that these gifts include the gift of knowledge; the gift of faith to be healed; the gift of prophecy; the gift of working miracles; the gift of speaking with tongues; and the gift of discerning spirits. A patriarchal blessing often instructs its recipient about one or more spiritual gifts that he or she possesses.

While the highest and most holy purpose of these gifts is to enable individuals to receive exaltation and return in glory to a loving Heavenly Father, a spiritual gift is part of the birthright of each participant in the adventure of mortality. That gift is available to men and women whether or not they choose

---

6 Marion G. Romney, "The Light of Christ," *Ensign*, May 1977.
7 See Boyd K. Packer, "The Light of Christ" (from an address given on June 22, 2004, at a seminar for new mission presidents, Missionary Training Center, Provo, Utah), *Ensign*, Apr. 2005.

to enter into covenants with God; every individual, and not just those who belong to The Church of Jesus Christ of Latter-day Saints, is the recipient of at least one spiritual gift. My father, Kenneth Hutchins, is a wonderful example of this truth. After his conversion in 1968, at age twenty-seven, he received a patriarchal blessing in which he was taught that he possessed the gift of faith to be healed. That gift has been manifested repeatedly in his years as a member of the Church; his body has miraculously recovered from gunshot wounds, three different bouts of cancer, a stroke, and many other potentially debilitating ailments. But my father would tell you that he experienced similar moments of healing in his youth (including his recovery from broken bones that resulted from jumping off a bridge and out of the path of an oncoming train), well before he was taught the message of the Restoration or baptized a member of The Church of Jesus Christ of Latter-day Saints. William Wordsworth wrote that we enter mortality "trailing clouds of glory," and that glory is partially manifest in the spiritual gifts that are the birthright of every man and woman.[8]

To "always remember" that a loving Heavenly Father has endowed the human family with spiritual gifts is to recall a premortal existence spent cultivating those gifts under His tutelage, in preparation for the challenges of this life. Elder Bruce R. McConkie taught that "all the spirits of men, while yet in the Eternal Presence, developed aptitudes, talents, capacities, and abilities of every sort, kind, and degree. During the long expanse of life which then was, an infinite variety of talents and abilities came into being."[9] To recognize a spiritual gift in ourselves or in others is to catch a glimpse of one's premortal identity and purpose. The Prophet Joseph Smith declared, "Whatever principle of intelligence we attain unto in this life, it will rise with us in the resurrection. And if a person gains more knowledge and intelligence in this life through his diligence and obedience than another, he will have so much the advantage in the world to come" (D&C 130:18–19). So, too, some of the spiritual gifts we enjoy in this life have risen with us from the world that was and into mortality, where we may, through the Spirit of Christ, continue to be instructed in their use and acquisition.

Our efforts to cultivate an extant spiritual gift or to seek after new aptitudes must begin with the foundational directive to "always remember" our Savior

---

[8] William Wordsworth, "Ode: Intimations of Immortality from Recollections of Early Childhood," in *The Poetical Works of William Wordsworth* (London: Edward Moxon, 1847), 441.

[9] Bruce R. McConkie, *The Mortal Messiah: From Bethlehem to Calvary*, 4 vols. (Salt Lake City: Deseret Book, 1979–81), 1:23.

and the gifts He has given us. Put more plainly, we must begin by honoring the sacramental covenant to remember Him always. Keeping that covenant is a minimum standard we must meet before we can reasonably ask for further help from heaven; we cannot expect to receive new light and knowledge from God unless and until we have embraced that which is already available to us.

How, then, can we better keep our commitment to always remember Jesus Christ? Daniel Kahneman won recognition from the Nobel committee at least in part for distinguishing between two different forms of human cognition, which he refers to as System 1 and System 2. System 1 is always running in the back of our brains; it processes our surroundings effortlessly and helps us make decisions instinctively through pattern recognition. When we see a stranger and conclude, from the expression on his face, that he is a grumpy man—that is System 1 in action. We do not need to think about the meaning of his downturned mouth; our brain has seen that pattern of facial muscles before and reaches a conclusion about its implications without any conscious effort on our part. System 2, on the other hand, requires mental exertion of the sort we make when solving a difficult math problem in our heads or memorizing a list of names. Only a sustained act of will enables us to focus on and, eventually, complete such tasks. Keeping our sacramental covenant to always remember the Redeemer will necessarily begin as a System 2 challenge, but none of us has the mental endurance to flex our mental System 2 muscles twenty-four hours a day. Our ability to "always remember" Jesus and the gifts He has given us, then, depends on moving that mental work from System 2 (conscious, effortful thinking) to System 1 (instinctive, effortless thinking).

In His Sermon on the Mount, Jesus warned, "No man can serve two masters," and that admonition applies to our mental processes as well as the actions of our body (Matthew 6:24). Indeed, Samuel the Lamanite reminds us that we can "always remember" only one thing at a time. Condemning the Nephites for their avarice, he declared, "Ye do not remember the Lord your God in the things with which he hath blessed you, but ye do always remember your riches, not to thank the Lord your God for them; yea, your hearts are not drawn out unto the Lord, but they do swell with great pride, unto boasting" (Helaman 13:22). Similarly, many of us are so concerned with the acquisition of wealth and social standing that we track financial opportunities and status symbols constantly with instinctive, System 1 thinking; we automatically search for and process social cues (hairstyle, clothing, jewelry, shoes) that indicate rank and riches. Like the Nephites condemned by Samuel, we may think of God and His blessings only occasionally, when sermons or other, external reminders prompt conscious, effortful System 2 thinking. Although our Father in Heaven can listen and respond to the prayers of billions simultaneously, our brains can only cope with one thought at a time; "my thoughts are not your thoughts, neither are your ways my ways, saith the Lord" (Isaiah 55:8). No man can serve two thoughts, and so our first attempts to always remember Jesus must begin with the choice to make Him the singular object of our attention. If we "always remember [our] riches," we cannot possibly always remember Him. We must "look unto [Him] in every thought" (D&C 6:36).

Doing this will be difficult, at least in part because the speed and complexity of life in the twenty-first century conspires to fracture our attention and divide our efforts. Each of us seeks to balance multiple, competing priorities on a daily basis, but that balancing act can make it challenging to discern which of our multiple tasks are essential and which are merely distractions siphoning time and attention from our service of the Master. Noting our struggle to balance competing objectives, Greg McKeown writes, "The word *priority* came into the English language in the 1400s. It was singular. It meant the very first or prior thing. It stayed singular for the next five hundred years. Only in the 1900s did we pluralize the term and start talking about *priorities*. Illogically, we reasoned that by changing the word we could bend reality. Somehow we would now be able to have multiple 'first' things."[10] There can only be one "first thing" in our life, and if we are to fulfill the measure of our creation, that first thing must be the Alpha and Omega of eternity, Jesus Christ.

During His mortal ministry, the Light of the World urged His disciples to make the acquisition of light and truth their singular priority. He taught, "The light of the body is the eye: if therefore thine eye be single, thy whole body shall be full of light" (Matthew 6:22). Kahneman's work on effortful and sustained System 2 thinking helps to clarify the implications of this teaching. In his laboratory, Kahneman discovered that "the pupils are sensitive indicators of mental effort. . . . During a mental multiplication, the pupil normally dilated to a large size within a few seconds and stayed large as long as the individual kept working on the problem; it contracted immediately when she found a solution or gave up."[11] The size of the pupil dictates how much light an eye receives; thus, optometrists who use eye drops to dilate a patient's eyes often distribute sunglasses to prevent the patient from being

---

10 Greg McKeown, *Essentialism; The Disciplined Pursuit of Less* (New York: Crown Business, 2014), 16.
11 Kahneman, *Thinking, Fast and Slow*, 32–33.

blinded by the additional light his or her eyes absorb in that condition. The sustained effort of System 2 thinking dilates our eyes and allows our physical bodies to perceive more of the light that surrounds us.

Kahneman's experiments provide a new perspective on the Savior's exhortation to let "thine eye be single." Embracing this invitation is a matter of effort and not merely orientation. It is not enough, in other words, simply to face the Light—although that is a good and necessary first step. Making our eye(s) single to His glory requires that we expend mental energy in pondering the perfections of Jesus Christ and seeking ways to apply that understanding in our lives. Only as we engage in effortful, System 2 thinking will we enjoy pupil-dilating and soul-expanding opportunities to receive further light and knowledge from our Father in Heaven.

In the context of our sacramental covenants, this means that it is not enough simply to mentally repeat, over and over again, the name of Jesus Christ. Such a practice might fulfill our obligation to always remember the Master, but it is also a minimal effort on our part—hardly the sort of mental work that would dilate our pupils and leave our bodies "full of light." If our efforts to remember the Redeemer are to be meaningful, they must also be effortful.

During the administration of the sacrament, effortful remembering might entail mentally responding to questions such as the following: Why do we use bread as a symbol of the Savior's body, and what do the scriptures teach us about the symbolic significance of bread? What would it mean to take the Savior's name upon us, and by what names is He known? Which of the Savior's bodies do we remember when we take the sacrament, and what is the significance to us of each? Do we remember the fragile body He arrived with as a baby? The adolescent body He learned to master as He "received grace for grace" (D&C 93:12)? The body of a carpenter working dawn to dusk to support an aging mother? The body "bruised, broken, torn for us" at Gethsemane and then on Calvary?[12] The resurrected body He displayed to disciples in Jerusalem and then the Americas? Answering these questions begins with memory but quickly moves to the more complex cognitive work of interpretation as we consider the import of relevant scriptural passages. When we ponder questions such as these, we invite instruction from the Holy Ghost, who "shall teach you all things, and bring all things to your remembrance" (John 14:26). His teaching will sanctify our bodies and fill us with light; our capacity to "always

---

12 "Jesus of Nazareth, Savior and King," *Hymns*, no. 181. Elder Claudio R. M. Costa provided a similar list of moments that we might remember from the Savior's life in his October 2015 general conference address, "That They Do Always Remember Him."

remember" is stimulated in fulfillment of the promise that we "may always have his Spirit to be with" us (D&C 20:77).

The same process of effortful remembering can facilitate our pursuit of spiritual gifts. We might begin by simply listing each of the thirteen spiritual gifts identified in section 46 of the Doctrine and Covenants:

- The gift of knowing, by the Holy Ghost, that Jesus Christ is the Son of God (46:13)
- The gift of believing on the words of those who know that Jesus is the Christ (46:14)
- The gift of knowing "the differences of administration" (46:15)
- The gift of knowing "the diversities of operations" (46:16)
- The gift of "the word of wisdom" (46:17)
- The gift of "the word of knowledge" (46:18)
- The gift of faith to be healed (46:19)
- The gift of faith to heal (46:20)
- The gift of working miracles (46:21)
- The gift of prophesying (46:22)
- The gift of discerning spirits (46:23)
- The gift of speaking with tongues (46:24)
- The gift of interpreting tongues (46:25)

Not every spiritual gift is included in this list; the gift of beholding angels and ministering spirits, for example, is included in Moroni's list of gifts but not in the Doctrine and Covenants (see Moroni 10:14).

Many spiritual gifts are never identified as such in scripture, but part of our responsibility to know "what those gifts are" entails recognizing them as such. To that end, in a 1987 general conference address, Elder Marvin J. Ashton identified a number of additional gifts:

> Let us review some of these less-conspicuous gifts: the gift of asking; the gift of listening; the gift of hearing and using a still, small voice; the gift of being able to weep; the gift of avoiding contention; the gift of being agreeable; the gift of avoiding vain repetition; the gift of seeking that which is righteous; the gift of not passing judgment; the gift of looking to God for guidance; the gift of being a disciple; the gift of caring for others; the gift of being able to ponder; the gift of offering prayer; the gift of bearing a mighty testimony; and the gift of receiving the Holy Ghost.[13]

---

13 Marvin J. Ashton, "There Are Many Gifts," *Ensign*, Nov. 1987.

This list expands our understanding of the aptitudes made available to us through the Spirit, but it is no more comprehensive than the lists in the Doctrine and Covenants and the Book of Mormon. To wit: in a 2017 general conference address, Elder John C. Pingree Jr. described still more gifts, including "having compassion, expressing hope, relating well with people, organizing effectively, speaking or writing persuasively, teaching clearly, and working hard."[14] Still other spiritual gifts might be mentioned, such as the gift of appreciating beauty, the gift of bearing testimony through music, and so on. Our capacity to remember and seek after these spiritual gifts is, accordingly, predicated on a willingness to learn about the full range of gifts a loving Father in Heaven has prepared for His children.

But just as our sacramental obligation to "always remember" the Savior requires more than the vain repetition of His name, our duty to "always remember . . . what those gifts are, that are given unto the church" involves greater effort on our part than the compilation and memorization of a list. Our remembrance of spiritual gifts should demand sustained System 2 thinking that will dilate our pupils and leave our bodies full of light. As with the sacrament, we might seek to answer questions about a specific spiritual gift, such as, "What episodes of healing are recorded in the scriptures, and how is the faith of those who are healed made manifest?" or we might consider more open-ended questions, like, "What spiritual gifts are manifest in the scriptural account of Nephi's search for food in the wilderness after he had broken his bow?" Pondering these and similar questions will invite the instruction of the Holy Ghost.

Unfortunately, the demands of life are such that we cannot devote our undivided time and attention to pondering these questions of eternal import all day, every day. In other words, even after we have begun to remember Jesus Christ and the gifts He has given for our benefit in a meaningful way, the problem of remembering *always* remains. System 2 thinking is effortful, and our capacity to exert mental effort is limited; we can increase that capacity, but not indefinitely. The only way to comply with a commandment to remember always is to shift the work of pondering from System 2 to System 1 so that we are constantly and unconsciously searching our surroundings for evidence of our Savior's love or for manifestations of the spiritual gifts with which He has endowed His children. Only when our remembering becomes instinctive can we keep this commandment with unwearyingness.

Social scientists suggest that effecting a transition from conscious to unconscious remembering can take as little as three weeks. Researchers have

---

[14] John C. Pingree Jr., "'I Have a Work for Thee,'" *Ensign* or *Liahona*, Nov. 2017.

demonstrated that spending just five minutes a day in conscious, effortful remembering can train our brains to automatically search the world around us for signs of the thing that we wish to remember. In one experiment, study participants were asked to write down three good things that happened to them each day. This process of effortful, System 2 thinking trained the System 1 portion of their brains to scan the world around them for good things so that the work of remembering positive experiences at the end of each day became easier and easier. Those who trained their unconscious selves to recognize and remember those good things, Shawn Achor explains, "were happier and less depressed at the one-month, three-month, and six-month follow-ups. . . . Even after stopping the exercise, they remained significantly happier and showed higher levels of optimism."[15] The small and simple task of consciously remembering three good things each day led study participants to be conscious of the good things around them always.

We can use the same process of active recollection in our efforts to make always remembering the Savior—and the gifts He has given us—an automatic and unconscious process. President Eyring attests that daily journaling, a small act of conscious remembrance, increased his ability to see the hand of God in his life:

> I wrote down a few lines every day for years. I never missed a day no matter how tired I was or how early I would have to start the next day. Before I would write, I would ponder this question: "Have I seen the hand of God reaching out to touch us or our children or our family today?" As I kept at it, something began to happen. As I would cast my mind over the day, I would see evidence of what God had done for one of us that I had not recognized in the busy moments of the day. As that happened, and it happened often, I realized that trying to remember had allowed God to show me what He had done.[16]

President Eyring made this small act of conscious remembrance a permanent part of his devotional practice, but social science research suggests that he would have retained a significant benefit even if he had stopped the experiment after a month. By training himself to scan the environment for evidence of God's gifts, he had moved the work of remembering from System 2 to System 1. With

---

15 Shawn Achor, *The Happiness Advantage: The Seven Principles of Positive Psychology that Fuel Success and Performance at Work* (New York: Crown Business, 2010), 101.

16 Henry B. Eyring, "O Remember, Remember," *Ensign* or *Liahona*, Nov. 2007.

that shift, President Eyring gained a greater ability to recognize and to always remember the gifts of God in his life.

In the Book of Mormon, Alma notes that this increased capacity to remember is a blessing associated with the keeping of records such as President Eyring's daily journal. As he entrusts his son Helaman with the writings of Nephite prophets, Alma explains that these records "have enlarged the memory of this people" (Alma 37:8), a blessing earnestly to be desired, given the imperative to "always remember." Written records enlarge our memory in ways both obvious and subtle. On the one hand, our brains simply cannot contain all the information included in dictionaries, encyclopedias, and other books, so written records work as an obvious extension of our memories: storage space for information we wish to reference without actively remembering. On the other hand, the act of keeping a record—of writing down facts, thoughts, and experiences—also expands our capacity to remember that information *without* the use of that record. In other words, keeping a record enlarges our ability to remember in subtle ways, by preserving our memory of specific facts, thoughts, and experiences more deeply and permanently in our consciousness. Even when we do not actively reference or re-read the words we write down, we remember and internalize what we have deliberately and thoughtfully recorded.

The consistent, conscious effort of three weeks can preserve in our minds a memory of how spiritual gifts have been made manifest and make us more attuned to their presence in our own lives or the lives of others. Consider spending five minutes each day prayerfully recording an answer to this question: What spiritual gifts have I seen manifest today in my own life or in the lives of others? This daily exercise will discipline our minds to search for and recognize gifts of the Spirit. Only when we have made the search for spiritual gifts a habit or routine will we fully obey the first and most fundamental duty as disciples of Jesus Christ: to "always remember him" (D&C 20:77) and, thus, to "always remember, and always retain in [our] minds what those gifts are, that [He has] given unto the church" (D&C 46:10).

CHAPTER 2
FOR WHAT THEY ARE GIVEN

IN EXHORTING MEMBERS OF THE Church to "seek ye earnestly the best gifts," the Lord warns of dangers associated with this pursuit. Lest His people "be seduced by evil spirits, or doctrines of devils, or the commandments of men," He stipulates that our striving must be motivated by an understanding of the purposes for which these gifts have been offered to the human family. Thus, those who strive to improve upon the aptitudes given each of us by God must do so while "always remembering for what they are given" (D&C 46:7–8). In other words, our receipt of a spiritual gift is partly predicated on our understanding of its purpose; you cannot fully receive or benefit from a gift whose use you do not understand.

This truth is wonderfully illustrated by the confusion my wife, Alana, and I experienced after the birth of our first child, Gabriel. Like many first-time parents, we sought to compensate for our inexperience by reading books on infant development, but despite our best efforts, we remained ignorant on some matters. In the midst of our preparations for Gabriel's arrival, one of our friends offered to throw a baby shower for Alana. We were grateful for the kindness of friends who prepared delicious food and purchased much-needed gifts that would help us care for our son. However, we also received several gifts that puzzled us, whose purpose we could not imagine.

One of Alana's friends gave us several bibs. These bibs were tiny and clearly intended to adorn the necks of newborns, but we knew that most infants do not begin consuming solid food for several months. Why, we asked ourselves, would a newborn baby need a bib? I had provided childcare for dozens of nieces and nephews, but I could not recall fastening a bib on any of them during their first months of life. We packed the bibs away in a drawer and hoped they would still fit our son when he started to eat solid food in six months.

In the weeks after Gabriel's birth, Alana and I entered a crash course in parenting. We constantly had to modify old habits and adopt new ones to meet his needs. We became expert problem solvers overnight—literally. As new parents quickly learn, an infant's most pressing needs inevitably arise between the hours of 2 and 4 a.m. One of the unexpected problems that confronted us was Gabriel's tendency to drool constantly and in large quantities. He drooled so much that he would soak entire outfits, and my vigilant wife would change him immediately, lest he catch cold. Because he sometimes drooled after we dosed him with a sugary, pink medicine, his clothes quickly became covered in pink stains. This drooling significantly increased the frequency with which we had to do laundry and left us feeling burdened.

A few weeks after Gabriel's birth, we attended a family reunion, where my wise sister-in-law Kelly, who has ten children of her own, noticed his drooling and asked, "Why don't you just put a bib on him?" Her question was revelatory. We immediately thought of the newborn-sized bibs carefully packed in a drawer and understood the purpose for which they had been given to us: they were intended not for Gabriel's eventual introduction to food but for the absorption of his drool. Once we understood their purpose, Alana and I removed the bibs from storage and used them constantly. The frequency with which we laundered Gabriel's clothes decreased, and we came to see his drooling as an endearing trait rather than a problem.

A gift that had previously been unappreciated was now used consistently and valued appropriately because we understood the intention of the giver and the purpose of the gift. Before Kelly's question revealed to us why we were given newborn-sized bibs, Alana and I had possessed much-needed gifts, yet we enjoyed none of their benefits. Only an understanding of the gifts' intended use allowed us to experience their positive impact in our lives.

As with the bibs given to us by thoughtful friends, many of the spiritual gifts offered to the human family by a wise and loving Father in Heaven are under-utilized or ignored because we fail to fully appreciate the purpose for which they were given. That purpose, Paul explains, is the promotion of unity and love between God's children. Immediately after his description of spiritual gifts made available through the Spirit of Christ, Paul declares that

> all these worketh that one and the selfsame Spirit, dividing to every man severally as he will. For as the body is one, and hath many members, and all the members of that one body, being many, are one body: so also is Christ. For by one Spirit

are we all baptized into one body, whether we be Jews or Gentiles, whether we be bond or free; and have been all made to drink into one Spirit. (1 Corinthians 12:11–13)

In Paul's metaphor, the possession of spiritual gifts differentiates individuals from one another, but their use also draws us closer together and unites us in a common purpose. Just as a hand differs from a foot and each limb enables our physical bodies to perform different tasks, so, too, the gift of working miracles differs from the gifts of healing, and each confers a different benefit to the human family, or the body of Christ.

The benefits conferred by these gifts to the body of Christ are complementary, just as the faculties of taste, touch, smell, sight, and hearing are complementary and provide different forms of sensory information to our bodies. The dispersal of spiritual gifts creates an incentive for individuals to draw nearer together in love so that each might receive the benefit of those spiritual gifts they do not yet possess. Each spiritual gift provides a different way of experiencing God's love and receiving the blessings He has prepared for us, just as each of the five senses provides a different avenue to experiencing the joys of the physical world. Nothing brings me sensory delight like a fresh apple pie, but my delight in that pie would be greatly diminished if I could experience it through only one of the five senses. The faculty of taste might seem a satisfactory lens through which to enjoy apple pie, but our tongues only process five basic tastes: sweet, bitter, salty, sour, and savory (umami). The complex flavors of apple pie à la mode—cinnamon, vanilla bean, the buttery taste of a perfect crust—can only be processed with the aid of our noses and a sense of smell. However, for many, the joy of delicious food is significantly compounded by the sight of that food and its texture; visual and tactile stimuli can significantly enhance the pleasure we take in a piece of apple pie. Each of the five senses enhances our experience of the physical world, and each of the spiritual gifts given us by God is meant to enhance our collective experience of His love.

Thus, Paul invites us to think of ourselves not as autonomous and self-sufficient individuals but as complementary pieces of a larger whole dependent on the goodwill and the unique talents of others. Because "all have not every gift given unto them" we are each, individually, like a body trying to enjoy the wonders of apple pie or another, similarly rich sensory experience through a single faculty (D&C 46:11). Thus, Paul asks, "If the whole body were an eye, where were the hearing? If the whole were hearing, where were the smelling?"

(1 Corinthians 12:17). We might ask, similarly—"If you possess the gift of the discerning of spirits, how will you enjoy the gift of working miracles or the gifts of healing?" Our receipt of the full range of blessings that a loving Heavenly Father has prepared for us is predicated on our willingness to become fully integrated into the body of Christ; we offer our own gifts in the service of others and receive, in turn, the benefit of their talents. Elder D. Todd Christofferson explains, "A major reason the Lord has a church is to create a community of Saints that will sustain one another in the 'strait and narrow path which leads to eternal life.' . . . This religion is not concerned only with self; rather, we are all called to serve. We are the eyes, hands, head, feet, and other members of the body of Christ."[1] Service, and the use of spiritual gifts on behalf of others, draws each member of the body of Christ together.

Isolated individuals cannot enjoy all of the gifts and blessings that a loving God desires to impart to His children, no matter how much time they spend in scripture study, prayer, and other forms of worship; a full measure of holiness and grace can only be experienced in community. As Terry Warner once observed in a Brigham Young University devotional, "We are not oysters or abalones, existing in shells—even though that is how we may feel when we become self-involved. We are members one of another, connected to each other, and especially to God, by spiritual sensitivities and obligations profound as eternity."[2] An oyster cannot appreciate the pearl it has cultivated; its sensitivity to an ingested grain of sand can only be admired and used by another. So, too, our spiritual gifts must be shared with and exercised on behalf of others in imitation of the Father, who gave His own pearl of great price to us.

This need for mutual reliance or interdependence is more clearly evident in other facets of the gospel. When, for example, we participate in vicarious ordinances for and in behalf of deceased family members, we acknowledge that "we without them cannot be made perfect; neither can they without us be made perfect" (D&C 128:18). Priesthood ordinances are administered, Alma taught, "in and through the atonement of the Only Begotten Son," as we sacrifice for and serve others in imitation of the Savior's example (Alma 13:5). Our ancestors sacrificed on our behalf, sharing the gift of mortality with us and laboring to provide us with physical bodies; we, in turn, share the gift of the gospel with them, entering into saving and exalting covenants on their behalf. This exchange of gifts by mutual sacrifice brings both parties closer to the glorious destiny prepared for us by a loving Heavenly Father.

---

1 D. Todd Christofferson, "Why the Church," *Ensign* or *Liahona*, Nov. 2015.

2 C. Terry Warner, "Honest, Simple, Solid, True" [Brigham Young University devotional, Jan. 16, 1996], speeches.byu.edu.

Similarly, when individuals enter the waters of baptism, they pledge "to bear one another's burdens" (Mosiah 18:8). That responsibility is most commonly understood as a commitment to bear the burdens of others, but there is a reciprocity implicit in the phrase that is often overlooked. When we agree to bear the burdens of others, we also commit to accept the help of others in carrying our own encumbrances; if everyone is willing to bear but no one is willing to share a burden, none of us can fulfill the measure of our creation. Thus, the baptismal covenant is a commitment both to share our spiritual gifts and to receive the spiritual gifts of others—that reciprocal exchange of gifts is an integral part of the process by which members of the body of Christ are made perfect.

In a charge to the men and women who left England to seek religious liberty in colonial North America, John Winthrop revisited Paul's vision of the body of Christ to stress the interdependence of disciples who enter into a covenantal relationship. "Among the members of the same body," Winthrop taught, "love and affection are reciprocal in a most equal and sweet kind of Commerce." This reciprocity is evident

> in the natural body [where] the mouth is at all the pains to receive, and mince the food which serves for the nourishment of all the other parts of the body, yet it hath not cause to complain; for first, the other parts send back by secret passages a due proportion of the same nourishment in a better form for the strengthening and comforting the mouth. Secondly the labor of the mouth is accompanied with such pleasure and content as far exceeds the pains it takes.[3]

The mouth's gift to the body, in this analogy, is an ability to prepare food so that it can be processed by the stomach. The stomach and other portions of the body thus benefitted then send the gift of energy, nutrients, and minerals back to the mouth. Winthrop wanted the colonists he sailed with to Massachusetts to recognize their mutual interdependence and then to draw closer together in love. He understood, with Paul, that "the whole body fitly joined together and compacted by that which every joint supplieth . . . maketh increase of the body unto the edifying of itself in love" (Ephesians 4:16). By promoting the unity, love, and interdependence of God's children, spiritual gifts stimulate the growth of Christ's body on earth.

Although we often speak of ourselves as members of the Church, we have forgotten the corporeal origins of that phrase. To call oneself a *member* is to acknowledge a reliance on the larger body, an incompleteness and inadequacy

---

[3] John Winthrop, "A Modell of Christian Charitie," in *Winthrop Papers*, vol. 2, ed. Stewart Mitchell (Boston: The Massachusetts Historical Society, 1931), 291–92.

when separated from the Church. If, for instance, I referred to myself not as a member of the Church but as a fingernail of the Church or a vein of the Church or a kidney of the Church, my interdependence on other members of the body of Christ might be more readily apparent. So, too, referring to ourselves in this way might emphasize the contribution that each individual makes to the body of Christ. A fingernail might seem insignificant, but as anyone who has ever lost a fingernail knows, it serves a vital function in protecting the nail bed and offers tremendous functionality in daily tasks such as gripping slippery objects or separating objects that are joined together. The body of Christ has a need of each and every individual and his or her gifts; one purpose of the Church is to place each member in contact with other members who have different, complementary gifts. Thus, when high priests groups were discontinued at the ward level and high priests were welcomed into larger elders quorums, Elder Ronald A. Rasband explained that one reason for the change was to establish "a greater diversity of gifts and capacities within the quorum."[4] Although the possession of a physical body provides everyone who is not literally connected at the hip (à la Chang and Eng, the famous Siamese twins) with an illusion of autonomy, the gospel diligently seeks to deconstruct such isolationism, thrusting us into contact and fellowship with others.

We are reminded constantly in scripture of our incompleteness and the need to be joined—sealed—to others. That is the message of Malachi's closing warning: "For, behold, the day cometh, that shall burn as an oven; and all the proud, yea, and all that do wickedly, shall be stubble: and the day that cometh shall burn them up, saith the Lord of hosts, that it shall leave them neither root nor branch" (Malachi 4:1). Malachi deploys an arboreal metaphor, comparing the unrighteous to tree trunks that will be severed from both roots (ancestors) and branches (posterity). Just as a tree trunk cut off from the minerals and moisture provided by its roots or the solar energy provided by its leaves is dead, incapable of growth, so, too, is a spiritual being cut off from other members of the body of Christ dead, incapable of growth. Thus Paul declares, "neither is the man without the woman, neither the woman without the man, in the Lord" (1 Corinthians 11:11). This requirement of interpersonal unity requires more than participation in sealing or marriage covenants; chastising the Latter-day Saints for their failure to care for the "poor and afflicted among them," the Lord declared that they "are not united according to the union required by the law of the celestial kingdom" (D&C 105:3–4). After the Savior's visit to the American continent, Lehi's descendants abandoned the distinctions of race

---

4 Ronald A. Rasband, "Behold! A Royal Army," *Ensign* or *Liahona*, May 2018.

and tribe. There were no "Lamanites, nor any manner of -ites; but they were in one" (4 Nephi 1:17). And in the current dispensation, while instructing the Saints to "let every man esteem his brother as himself," the Lord commanded, "Be one; and if ye are not one ye are not mine" (D&C 38:25, 27). Members of Christ's Church must recognize themselves as just that: members, or parts of a larger whole into which we strive to be fully integrated, relying on the capacities and gifts of others just as we ask them, in turn, to depend upon our affection and aptitudes.

The exercise of spiritual gifts both fosters and relies upon this sense of comm-*unity*. Although we tend to think of spiritual gifts as aptitudes pursued by an individual, they are better understood as a sort of team sport, in that the outcome or heavenly outpouring is contingent on the faith and gifts of two or more participants; the attempt to cultivate spiritual gifts is more like volleyball than golf, more like synchronized swimming than the high jump or a triathlon. Only through the combined efforts of multiple individuals are the full benefits of God's gifts to us realized. For this reason, many spiritual gifts identified in the scriptures are paired with a second, complementary gift to be exercised in conjunction or combination with the first: the gift of faith to heal and the gift of faith to be healed (see D&C 46:19–20); the gift of speaking in tongues and the gift of interpreting tongues (see D&C 46:24–25); the gift of knowing that Jesus is the Christ and the gift of believing on the words of those who know (see D&C 46:13–14). The collaborative use of complementary gifts provides the greatest benefit to the body of Christ, just as the collaborative use of multiple senses provides our bodies the most complete experience of this world in which we live.

Paul attests to the need for spiritual teamwork in his description of the gift of tongues. Following the example of Joseph Smith, modern prophets and Apostles encourage members of the Church to think of that gift as a form of divine aid in learning a foreign language.[5] But members of both the early

---

5 In an 1841 discourse reported by Willard Richards, Joseph Smith "remarked that the gift of Tongues was necessary in the church; <but> That if satan could not speak in tongues he could not tempt a Dutchman, or any other nation, but the English, for he can tempt the Englishman, for he has tempted me, & I am an Englishman; but the Gift of Tongues, by the power of the Holy Ghost, in the church, is for the benefit of the servants of God to preach to unbelievers, as on the days of Pentecost. when devout men from evry nation shall assemble to hear of the things of God. let the <elders> preach to them in their own Mother tongue. whither it is German, French, Spanish or Irish. or any other. & let those interpret who understand the tongue <Language> spoken. in their mother tongue. & this is what the Apostle meant. in

Christian and the Restoration-era Church regarded this gift differently, as the ability to reveal divine truths in words unintelligible to human ears. Thus Paul urges the Saints in Corinth to pursue the gift of prophecy, rather than the gift of tongues, because "he that speaketh in an unknown tongue speaketh not unto men, but unto God: for no man understandeth him; howbeit in the spirit he speaketh mysteries" (1 Corinthians 14:2). In the absence of understanding, Paul stipulates, the gift of tongues is of no value and has no place in the body of Christ: "But if there be no interpreter, let him keep silence in the church" (1 Corinthians 14:28). Only with the contributions of a second individual who possesses the gift of interpreting tongues does speaking in tongues benefit the ecclesiastical body; in the primitive Church, these complementary and interrelated gifts had to be exercised in tandem or not at all.

This principle should affect the manner in which we seek to exercise similar gifts today. When I was assigned to labor in Brazil as a missionary, I sought earnestly for the gift of tongues so that I could teach the gospel in Portuguese. I taught myself to read the language before entering the missionary training center by placing two copies of the Book of Mormon side by side: one in Portuguese and another in English. In the three months between when I received my call and when I was set apart as a full-time missionary, every prayer I offered expressed a desire that God would bless me with the gift of tongues. However, after arriving in Brazil, I came to realize two things in short order: first, an ability to read Portuguese would not allow me to speak the language; and second, I needed to understand what others were saying before I could rely on the gift of tongues to help me respond effectively. Immediately, then, I began to pray for the gift of interpreting tongues so that I could understand what others around me were trying to communicate. These efforts and the patient instruction of native speakers helped me quickly attain a degree of fluency.

But the process I undertook also illustrates a gross misunderstanding of gospel principles on my part. As a missionary, the ostensible purpose of my labors was to help others come closer to Christ, but my prayers seeking the gift of tongues and the gift of interpreting of tongues were inwardly focused; I was worried about *my* ability to communicate and *my* ability to understand the communication of others. In other words, I approached the problem as an individual rather than as a member of the body of Christ. Because communication is a team sport, in which success depends on the efforts of both a speaker and a

---

1s[t] corinthians 14.27" (Joseph Smith, "Discourse, 26 December 1841, as Reported by Willard Richards," in Book of the Law of the Lord [www.josephsmithpapers.org], 39).

listener, any petition for divine intervention should address the needs of both parties. Thus, when the Lord reveals a divine pattern for communication in the Doctrine and Covenants, He stipulates that the Spirit must magnify the efforts of each:

> Verily I say unto you, he that is ordained of me and sent forth to preach the word of truth by the Comforter, in the Spirit of truth, doth he preach it by the Spirit of truth or some other way? And if it be by some other way it is not of God. And again, he that receiveth the word of truth, doth he receive it by the Spirit of truth or some other way? If it be some other way it is not of God. (D&C 50:17–20)

Only when the efforts of both a speaker and a listener are magnified by the power of God do they truly "understand one another, and both are edified and rejoice together" (D&C 50:22). In seeking for myself the gifts of tongues and of interpreting tongues, my self-centered prayers were "looking beyond the mark" (Jacob 4:14). Those prayers would have been more efficacious if, instead of praying solely for myself, I had also asked that those who I interacted with might speak to me with the gift of tongues and receive the gift of interpreting my tongue.

The gospel of Jesus Christ reveals our interdependence in the work of salvation and exaltation, and we must exercise spiritual gifts in concert with others to achieve God's purposes, which cannot be fulfilled without the cooperation and mutual striving of two or more individuals. President M. Russell Ballard explained, "Just as a woman cannot conceive a child without a man, so a man cannot fully exercise the power of the priesthood to establish an eternal family without a woman. In other words, in the eternal perspective, both the procreative power and the priesthood power are shared by husband and wife."[6] The gift of creating life must be exercised jointly, by a man and woman acting together, and the administration of essential priesthood ordinances likewise requires either the participation of at least two priesthood holders or the confirming witness of observers that priesthood power was exercised appropriately. The appropriate exercise of these powers requires the collaboration of multiple individuals in the service of others: Husband and wife conceive and care for children together; priesthood holders prepare, bless, and pass the sacrament for the benefit of a congregation. Receiving or using a gift from God turns our focus outward. Elder David A. Bednar's description of the priesthood might profitably

---

6 M. Russell Ballard, "This Is My Work and My Glory," *Ensign* or *Liahona*, May 2013.

be applied to our understanding of both spiritual gifts and the procreative power: "Nothing about the priesthood is self-centered. The priesthood always is used to serve, to bless, and to strengthen other people."[7] So, too, spiritual gifts are intended to serve, to bless, and to strengthen other people; they turn our focus outward. Seeking spiritual gifts for selfish reasons offends God, and we should examine our motives for their acquisition searchingly.[8] In our efforts to develop and use spiritual gifts, we should always begin with a desire to bless and lift those within our circle of influence.

Even those gifts that seem primarily to benefit the individual who seeks them are best applied and most commonly received in the service of others. The gift of knowledge, for example, enables its possessor to obtain a "knowledge of things as they are, and as they were, and as they are to come. . . . a knowledge of history, and of countries, and of kingdoms, of laws of God and man" (D&C 93:24, 53). The most obvious beneficiary of that knowledge is the man or woman who seeks it, the recipient of the gift. But this gift, like all spiritual gifts, is most often received when the seeker expresses an intent to use the knowledge received in service of others. That principle is declared in the Doctrine and Covenants; God bequeaths "the word of knowledge, that all may be taught to be wise and to have knowledge" (46:18). Knowledge received from God or acquired with His help comes not, primarily, to satisfy the curiosity of an individual seeker. Rather, the Lord bestows the gift of knowledge to individuals who intend to teach others of what they have learned and facilitate the dispersal of truth.

This truth, that the gift of knowledge is given most readily and abundantly to those who will share what they have learned with others, is manifest each week in the words of speakers and teachers throughout the Church. Many who stand to speak in sacrament meeting or to teach a lesson in Sunday School begin their remarks by expressing gratitude for the opportunity to do so. They often share a conviction that the invitation to speak or to teach was inspired because they have learned so much more about the topic than they had gleaned

---

7 David A. Bednar, "The Powers of Heaven," *Ensign* or *Liahona*, May 2012.

8 As Elder Henry B. Eyring has testified, "If you want to receive the gifts of the Spirit, you have to want them for the right reasons. Your purposes must be the Lord's purposes. To the degree your motives are selfish, you will find it difficult to receive those gifts of the Spirit that have been promised to you. . . . God is offended when we seek the gifts of the Spirit for our own purposes rather than for His." Furthermore, "our selfish motives may not be obvious to us," and so we must ask the Lord to purify our hearts and our motives in prayer (Henry B. Eyring, "Gifts of the Spirit for Hard Times" [Brigham Young University devotional, Sept. 10, 2006], speeches.byu.edu).

from previous study and because what they have learned seems tailored to their individual needs and circumstances. This refrain, which I have heard hundreds of times in meetinghouses around the world, is so common because it expresses a fundamental truth: God gives the gift of knowledge first and most freely to those who will teach others of what they have learned. The speakers and teachers who report receiving inspiration, guidance, and the personal instruction of the Holy Ghost as they prepare their talks or lesson plans had often read the same material on earlier occasions, such as during personal scripture study, without a similar outpouring of understanding. But a commitment to share what will be learned with others authorizes the Holy Ghost to communicate additional light and truth; thus, the Lord commands His people,

> Teach ye diligently and my grace shall attend you, that you may be instructed more perfectly in theory, in principle, in doctrine, in the law of the gospel, in all things that pertain unto the kingdom of God, that are expedient for you to understand; of things both in heaven and in the earth, and under the earth; things which have been, things which are, things which must shortly come to pass; things which are at home, things which are abroad. (D&C 88:78–79)

Grace and the more perfect instruction of the Holy Ghost will come as we diligently prepare to teach that which we learn. Like with the gift of knowledge, each spiritual gift is given most abundantly to those who will share its fruits with others.

Because gifts of the spirit are provided for the purpose of drawing all members of the body of Christ closer together, the forty-sixth section of the Doctrine and Covenants begins with a series of stern warnings against insularity or cliquishness in the Church. Four times in as many verses of scripture, the Lord warns against any attempt to restrict or limit participation in meetings of the Church by those who seek its blessings:

- "Nevertheless ye are commanded never to cast any one out from your public meetings" (D&C 46:3).
- "Ye are also commanded not to cast any one who belongeth to the church out of your sacrament meetings" (D&C 46:4).
- "And again I say unto you, ye shall not cast any out of your sacrament meetings who are earnestly seeking the kingdom" (D&C 46:5).
- "If there be any that are not of the church, that are earnestly seeking after the kingdom, ye shall not cast them out" (D&C 46:6).

Scriptural instruction about the nature of spiritual gifts and how best to seek them is preceded by a prohibition on excluding any sincere worshipers from the meetings and blessings of the Church, suggesting that spiritual gifts must be sought in an attitude of service, outreach, and inclusion, for the edification of all. Few would consciously and deliberately exclude others from the blessings of Church fellowship, but whenever our political beliefs, personal prejudices, or insular affections make others feel unwelcome in our presence, we disqualify ourselves from exercising and receiving a full range of the gifts with which God wishes to bless us.

One of His primary purposes in endowing some with one gift and some with another is to foster in us a greater sense of our need for one another. Our interdependence is more evident on occasions or in situations that stretch us beyond what we might previously have thought of as our limits. Consider the example of Church members living on the outskirts of Cambridge, Massachusetts, during the late 1980s and early 1990s. These saints, living in Revere, Malden, and other surrounding communities, had to commute through crowded city streets each Sunday morning to arrive at their sacrament services in the Cambridge chapel; as a result, only a few of the hundreds of Church members living in these outlying towns attended regularly. Elder Kim B. Clark, who would later serve in the First Quorum of the Seventy and as the president of Brigham Young University-Idaho, was the bishop of the Cambridge First Ward at the time, and he challenged the fifteen members who regularly made this commute to form a branch, promising that they could obtain funding for their own space if sacrament meeting attendance grew to sixty. Kristen Smith Dayley recounts that each week, members of the branch would set up twenty chairs. After the service, those in attendance would reach out to individuals who might have filled the five empty chairs and ask, "Are you okay? Is there anything we can do for you? Do you think you could come next week? Because we really need you." Once the branch filled twenty chairs, they set up an additional twenty chairs and reached out to a new group of saints, expressing a need for their fellowship and faith. According to this pattern, that group of fifteen grew within eight years to a congregation of more than one hundred, and a chapel was built in Revere, Massachusetts, to accommodate this expanding body of saints.[9] Underlying this period of remarkable growth was a deep awareness, on the part of those who formed the original branch, of their need for the presence and talents of those not already attending. We cannot afford to cast anyone out

---

9 Kristen Smith Dayley, *For All the Saints: Lessons Learned in Building the Kingdom* (Springville, UT: CFI, 2012), 163.

of our sacrament meetings—or even to casually neglect those who are or who could have been in our sacrament meetings—because we desperately need their insights, faith, and gifts in the body of Christ, just as a mouth or digestive tract needs eyes to see and hands to gather food before it can nourish the rest of the body. We may not initially recognize the gifts or capacities that others have to offer, and so we may not know *why* we need their contributions—but we do.

The role of Jaime Valarezo in facilitating the growth of another branch that began as a dependent unit of the Cambridge First Ward illustrates the role that one individual's spiritual gifts might play in enlarging the body of Christ. In 1976, recognizing a need for priesthood leadership if the ward's small group of Spanish-speaking sisters was ever to become an independent congregation, a joint fast was held by these sisters, asking God to send them a strong priesthood leader who would draw other priesthood holders into the branch. That very Sunday, Valarezo, a teenager, illegal immigrant, and recent convert with a debilitating stutter, walked into their chapel. Those who had fasted were disappointed, skeptical that this very young man with a speech impediment could provide the leadership for which they had petitioned the Lord. But when the local missionaries took Jaime on splits, they discovered that he had the gift of caring for children:

> Jaime had a natural affinity for children and the children enjoyed their time with him so much that they begged their parents to return to "Jaime's church." Eventually the entire family was baptized. Soon Jaime was spending hours at the Cambridge building, tending to the needs of young boys and girls as the missionaries taught mothers and fathers in back-to-back appointments. With Jaime's assistance, the missionaries were able to make more appointments and teach more effectively. Very quickly the dependent Spanish branch began out-baptizing all other units in the stake, averaging two to three baptisms a week.[10]

In large part because of Valarezo's missionary efforts, the Cambridge Stake grew to host three Spanish-speaking units; his unique ability to gain the love and trust of children was a spiritual gift enabling the miraculous growth that sisters of the branch had prayed for. Because they recognized their need for the gifts of others and chose not to reject or figuratively cast out a young man whose "outward appearance" was unimpressive, they reaped the benefits of his divinely endowed love for small children (1 Sam. 16:7).

---

10 Dayley, *For All the Saints*, 74.

Both as individuals and as an ecclesiastical body, we will only enjoy a fullness of the spiritual gifts that a loving Heavenly Father has provided to the human family if we recognize and value the capacities of all those in our midst, rejecting the temptation to ignore, undervalue, or marginalize those whose talents we desperately need. Because so many spiritual gifts are complementary, they must be exercised in conjunction with one another, drawing together individuals who might otherwise have remained aloof or disengaged. As we embrace our various roles as members of the body of Christ and exercise our spiritual gifts in the service of others, the Church grows and is strengthened. This is the purpose for which spiritual gifts have been given: to draw our hearts together in love.

CHAPTER 3
HAVE MIRACLES CEASED?

THE BEST-KNOWN OUTPOURING OF SPIRITUAL gifts came almost two thousand years ago, shortly after the death, resurrection, and ascension of Jesus Christ. As He prepared the remaining eleven Apostles for His departure, the Savior instructed them that He would "send the promise of my Father upon you: but tarry ye in the city of Jerusalem, until ye be endued with power from on high" (Luke 24:49). In the book of Acts, Luke records that this promise was fulfilled on the day of Pentecost, a feast commemorating Moses's reception of the law on Mount Sinai. Each year, the children of Israel celebrated this event on the fiftieth day of Passover. (We refer to this celebration as Pentecost because the Greek *pentekoste* means fiftieth.)[1] On this occasion, seven weeks after the death of Christ,

> when the day of Pentecost was fully come, [the Apostles] were all with one accord in one place. And suddenly there came a sound from heaven as of a rushing mighty wind, and it filled all the house where they were sitting. And there appeared unto them cloven tongues like as of fire, and it sat upon each of them. And they were all filled with the Holy Ghost, and began to speak with other tongues, as the Spirit gave them utterance. (Acts 2:1–4)

This dramatic manifestation of spiritual gifts came to a group of disciples unified—"with one accord in one place"—by their desire to fulfill Christ's commission "that repentance and remission of sins should be preached in his name among all nations" (Luke 24:47). And the outcome or effect of this outpouring was to

---

1 On the relationship between Pentecost and Sinai, see Martin C. Salter, *The Power of Pentecost: An Examination of Acts 2:17–21* (Eugene, OR: Resource Publications, 2012), 28–30.

draw together the hearts of many, as thousands of those in attendance, from nations throughout the known world, accepted the Apostles' testimony of Christ and received the saving ordinances of baptism by water and by the Holy Ghost. These early members of the body of Christ cultivated an ethos of unity and love that John Winthrop and other Christian reformers would strive to recapture throughout the centuries: "all that believed were together, and had all things common; and sold their possessions and goods, and parted them to all men, as every man had need. . . . with gladness and singleness of heart" (Acts 2:44–46).

Although many Christians have sought to recreate the selfless and single-minded community of saints described in Acts, these attempts have always ended in failure; the early Church was uniquely successful in establishing a sustainable, consecrated community. Similarly, the dramatic and public display of spiritual gifts leading to their formation of this community was a singular event in sacred history. Only the experiences of Nephi and Lehi in Helaman 5, as they were encircled with heavenly fire in a Lamanite prison and converted thousands, or of the Latter-day Saints who participated in the Kirtland temple dedication, seem comparable (see Helaman 5:21–50). Indeed, the public and visible exercise of spiritual gifts is such an unusual occurrence in Christian history that many Protestant reformers during the Renaissance regarded the exercise of spiritual gifts with suspicion and skepticism. To paraphrase Mormon, they believed that miracles ceased shortly after Christ ascended into heaven and sat down on the right hand of God—that spiritual gifts had been given to the Apostles and to other members of a founding generation but that such things had since been done away (see Moroni 7:27).

Protestant leaders offered different explanations for this decline in spiritual gifts. John Wesley, whose followers came to be known as Methodists, characterized the disappearance of spiritual gifts as one of the signs of the Second Coming identified by Jesus Christ during His mortal ministry: "It does not appear that these extraordinary gifts of the Holy Ghost were common in the church for more than two or three centuries. . . . The real cause of it was, 'the love of many,' almost of all Christians, so called, was 'waxed cold.' The Christians had no more of the Spirit of Christ than the other Heathens" (Matthew 24:12).[2] One of Winthrop's contemporaries, John Cotton, offered a different explanation, arguing that spiritual gifts had been bestowed for the purpose of establishing the Church and converting thousands during the early days of apostolic government. He acknowledged that New Testament Christians "had allowance

---

2 John Wesley, "Sermon LXXXIX: The More Excellent Way," *The Works of the Rev. John Wesley*, vol. 7, 4th ed. (London: John Mason, 1840), 25.

from the Church to employ their gifts to the public edification of the Church. But as such gifts now are not ordinarily bestowed, (which were at first given chiefly for admiration and conviction of Infidels, 1 Cor. 14:22) so we would not call upon men now, to prefer their ordinary common gift."[3] Members of The Church of Jesus Christ of Latter-day Saints who are familiar with accounts of the miraculous and public exercise of spiritual gifts during the early days of the Restoration might similarly conclude that "such gifts now are not ordinarily bestowed" and that now the Church has been well established, we have only the capacity to exercise an "ordinary common gift."

Extraordinary accounts of publicly exercised spiritual gifts abound in the annals of early Church history. When, as a new convert, Brigham Young first met the Prophet Joseph Smith, he was invited to pray. As Brigham opened his mouth to speak, he fell under the influence of the Holy Ghost, and those present heard him speak in tongues. Joseph identified the words he spoke as "the pure Adamic language," and this gift was made manifest in similarly dramatic fashion during many public meetings of the early Church.[4] Then, at the dedication of the Kirtland Temple in 1836, Latter-day Saints experienced a modern manifestation of gifts reminiscent of the Pentecost miracle. Joseph Smith wrote, "a voice was heard like the sound of a rushing mighty wind which filled the Temple and all the congregation simultaneously arose being moved upon by an invisible power many began to speak in Tongues and prophecy."[5] Forty years later, Orson Pratt would add his witness that "God was there, his angels were there, the Holy Ghost was in the midst of the people . . . and they were filled from the crown of their heads to the soles of their feet with the power and inspiration of the Holy Ghost, and uttered forth prophecies in the midst of that congregation, which have been fulfilling from that day to the present time."[6] Just as the miracles witnessed on the day of Pentecost brought about the conversion of thousands, a public exercise of spiritual gifts during the Kirtland Temple dedication similarly strengthened the faith of many hundreds.

These public manifestations of miraculous gifts during two different foundational periods of Church history help to shape our sense of what spiritual

---

3 John Cotton, *Singing of Psalmes a Gospel-Ordinance* (London: 1647), 16.
4 John G. Turner, *Brigham Young: Pioneer Prophet* (Cambridge, MA: Harvard University Press, 2012), 32.
5 Joseph Smith, *History*, 1836–1838, volume B-1, p. 3, www.josephsmithpapers.org.
6 Orson Pratt, "On the Dedication of the New Tabernacle," in *Journal of Discourses*, 18.132.

gifts are and how they should operate in our lives. Unfortunately, these well-known episodes are so different from our own, individual experiences of spiritual gifts that they may also work to sow doubt about the divinity of those gifts exercised and observed in our day. Small wonder that Mormon, writing for our day, asks, "Have miracles ceased?" (Moroni 7:29). Each of us must grapple with and answer the question of why extraordinary demonstrations of God's power and gifts might seem so much rarer today than in the apostolic Church or in the early years of the Restoration.

Fortunately, Mormon's own life provides a helpful paradigm for thinking through this question. Living several hundred years after the Savior restored His Church among Lehi's descendants, Mormon witnessed an erosion of faith in Jesus Christ and the disappearance of those gifts made available through His Spirit. Immediately after the Savior's visit to the Americas, descendants of Lehi enjoyed a period of spiritual prosperity comparable to that which the apostolic Church experienced during Pentecost. They too "had all things common among them; therefore there were not rich and poor, bond and free, but they were all made free, and partakers of the heavenly gift" (4 Nephi 1:3). These heavenly gifts were exercised in abundance: "there were great and marvelous works wrought by the disciples of Jesus, insomuch that they did heal the sick, and raise the dead, and cause the lame to walk, and the blind to receive their sight, and the deaf to hear; and all manner of miracles did they work" (4 Nephi 1:5). When Mormon was born, the restoration of Christ's Church and the public, miraculous exercise of spiritual gifts was a matter of recent history. In this respect, Mormon confronted circumstances similar to those facing Latter-day Saints in the twenty-first century.

We, like Mormon, are only a few hundred years removed from a time of spectacularly public spiritual manifestations, when "there were mighty miracles wrought among the disciples of Jesus" (4 Nephi 1:13). In addition to the spiritual gifts exercised during the Kirtland temple dedication, we might point to accounts of mass healing in Nauvoo; Brigham Young attested that in 1839, as the Saints suffered from malaria and other mosquito-borne illnesses,

> Joseph arose from his bed of sickness, and the power of God rested upon him. He commenced in his own house and dooryard, commanding the sick, in the name of Jesus Christ, to arise and be made whole, and they were healed according to his word. He then continued to travel from house to house and from tent to tent upon the bank of the river, healing the sick as he went.[7]

---

[7] Brigham Young, *The Journal of Brigham: Brigham Young's Own Story in His Own Words*, ed. Leland R. Nelson (Provo, UT: Council Press, 1980), 23.

When a local man unaffiliated with the Church heard that Joseph possessed the faith to heal and that the Saints had faith to be healed, he told the Prophet of his sick children and asked for aid. Wilford Woodruff remembers that Joseph instructed him, "'You go with this man and heal his children,' at the same time giving me a red silk handkerchief, and said, 'After you lay hands upon them, wipe their faces with it, and they shall be healed.' . . . I went and did as I was commanded, and the children were healed."[8] At a time when the general populace regards accounts of the supernatural with skepticism, such stories may seem fabulous—more folktale than fact. Like Latter-day Saints in the twenty-first century, who must grapple with the question of why the miracles of recent Church history no longer seem to occur with regularity, Mormon was familiar with stories of spiritual gifts exercised publicly and in dramatic fashion by those living just a few hundred years before him.

These miraculous and public demonstrations of God's power in Kirtland and Nauvoo took place during a period of American history known as the Second Great Awakening, a time of religious zeal characterized by mass conversions and a widespread expectation that the Second Coming was imminent. Faith in Jesus Christ was widespread, almost universal. But Mormon lived in a time more like our own, when a faith that had been rekindled in the recent past was failing. Even before Mormon's birth, the descendants of Lehi "began to be proud in their hearts, because of their exceeding riches, and become vain" (4 Nephi 1:43). Prosperity, pride, and vanity led to other sins, and Mormon makes a causal link between this failure of faith and the disappearance of spiritual gifts. He laments that "wickedness did prevail upon the face of the whole land, insomuch that the Lord did take away His beloved disciples, and the work of miracles and of healing did cease because of the iniquity of the people. And there were no gifts from the Lord" (Mormon 1:13–14). When the Nephites and Lamanites collectively abandoned their belief in Jesus Christ and in His gospel, their right to exercise those spiritual gifts given by the Spirit of God to every man was revoked (see D&C 46:11). As a result of sin and unbelief, the day of miracles—of publicly exercised gifts—ceased (see Moroni 7:35–37).

Mormon dwells at some length on his efforts to persuade his friends and neighbors and acquaintances to repent of their sins. He "did endeavor to preach unto this people" in his youth (Mormon 1:16), and his "soul had been poured out in prayer unto my God all the day long for them" (Mormon 3:12). Surely if they had responded to his ministry and repented, a loving Heavenly Father

---

8 Wilford Woodruff, "History of Wilford Woodruff," *Millennial Star*, May 1865, 326.

would have restored their capacity to draw on the powers of heaven and exercise spiritual gifts; with repentance, our access to these gifts, like our access to other blessings made available through the merits and mercies of Jesus Christ, can return over the course of time, as we are sanctified through His atoning grace. But notwithstanding Mormon's best efforts, the people of his day "willfully rebelled against their God" (Mormon 1:16). Because of their sinfulness, their ability to use and cultivate spiritual gifts was suspended.

Mormon's sobering declaration that in his day "there were no gifts" might serve as both an explanation and a warning for Latter-day Saints, who live in a time foreseen by prophets. Mormon's son, Moroni, testified that "Jesus Christ hath shown you unto me," and these two were specially prepared for the work of compiling the Book of Mormon for modern readers by virtue of their experience with a people who rejected the Savior "to boast in their own strength" (Mormon 8:35; 3:9). For those who wonder why the Church no longer observes regular public demonstrations of spiritual gifts, Mormon's record might serve as one important explanation. In his day, a prevailing culture of doubt and skepticism constrained the Spirit of God and prevented the public exercise of spiritual gifts despite the individual faith of Mormon and those like him, who retained their belief in the Redeemer. Mormon and Moroni believed in God and in His power with surety; they received, in private, the ministering of angels. But because of His commitment to maintaining the agency of His children, our Father in Heaven rarely allows the faith of the righteous to constrain the active disbelief of others, and neither Mormon nor Moroni was permitted to use his spiritual gifts publicly. The pride and determined disbelief of his people made it impossible for Mormon to call on the powers of heaven in a way that would have led to meaningful change. God created Adam and each of his descendants to "be agents unto themselves" (D&C 29:39), and Mormon's people were not merely "to be acted upon" by his faith but could act for themselves, rejecting his teachings and the Spirit's entreaties in a way that limited his capacity to exercise spiritual gifts on their behalf (2 Nephi 2:14). "God will force no man to heaven," and we may not force those without faith to receive the fruits of our spiritual gifts.[9]

Accordingly, Mormon's declaration that "there were no gifts" helps to explain why spiritual gifts might not be manifested publicly in a given age or location—their exercise is contingent on the faith and the agency of those present. This

---

9 The hymn that Latter-day Saints sing as "Know This, That Every Soul is Free" was originally published with the title "Freedom of the Human Will"; see in Elias Smith and Abner Jones, *Hymns, Original and Selected, for the Use of Christians*, 3rd edition (Exeter, MA: 1809), 225.

truth is similarly demonstrated by the Savior's example in healing the daughter of Jairus, "one of the rulers of the synagogue" (Mark 5:22). As Jesus journeyed to his house, the ruler's daughter died, and messengers told Jairus that he need not trouble the Master any further. But Jesus reassured Jairus that all would be well and pressed forward, allowing "no man to follow him, save Peter, and James, and John" (Mark 5:37). When He arrived at the house and told Jairus that "the damsel is not dead, but sleepeth," those who had gathered—presumably to mourn her passing—"laughed him to scorn" (Mark 5:39–40). Nevertheless, Jesus persisted. As He had already done *en route* to the house, Jesus winnowed away the crowd that had gathered to watch Him perform some great miracle, allowing only Jairus and his wife to enter the room where their daughter lay and witness His healing ministrations. In removing all from the house but His three most faithful Apostles and the parents of the girl He would heal, Jesus cultivated an atmosphere of belief that made her return to life possible. On other occasions and in other places, Mark records, when the Savior was surrounded by a culture of unbelief, "he could there do no mighty work," constrained by the doubt of those He might otherwise have helped (Mark 6:5–6; see Matthew 13:58). The apostolic record of Christ's life makes it clear that the exercise of spiritual gifts is contingent on the faith of those who would witness or benefit from their use; for God to work miracles in the face of active disbelief would be to ignore the agency of those who choose not to believe in Him or His power. Thus, a culture shaped by skeptics and unbelievers, such as that encountered by Mormon and prevalent in our own day, might prevent the exercise of spiritual gifts unless in a private setting, where the faith of those invited to be present will facilitate the work of God and fortify all present.

While every individual enters mortality possessing one or more spiritual gifts, Mormon's account reminds readers that these gifts, like other blessings we might seek, "are made conditional on our asking for them" and "require some work or effort on our part before we can obtain them" (Bible Dictionary, "Prayer"). Mormon records that he "was visited of the Lord" in his youth and enjoyed heavenly ministrations (Mormon 1:15). These experiences and his receipt of spiritual gifts led him to desire that others might similarly enjoy the fruits of the gospel. Having been "given by the Holy Ghost to know that Jesus Christ is the Son of God" (D&C 46:13), Mormon "did endeavor to preach unto this people" (Mormon 1:16) and exercise a second gift to "teach the word of knowledge" (Moroni 10:10). Mormon labored to cultivate a new gift for the best possible reason—a love of God and of humankind—but failed through no fault of his own. Although he attempted to share the knowledge he had gained with others, Mormon writes that "my mouth was shut, and I was forbidden that I should preach unto them; for behold they had wilfully rebelled against their God" (Mormon 1:16). His short-lived effort to preach and the spiritual degeneration of his people should serve as a twofold warning.

First, Mormon's experience is both a reminder that spiritual gifts are just that—gifts—and a caution against any presumption of entitlement on the part of recipients. Because we are encouraged to "seek ye earnestly the best gifts" (D&C 46:8) and because such seeking often entails sustained study or effort on our part, we may inadvertently come to think of spiritual gifts as self-developed talents rather than manifestations of grace magnifying our natural capacities and best efforts. For example, when missionaries are called to speak a foreign language, their prayers for the gift of tongues are always accompanied by long hours of study as they seek to master the intricacies of Korean syntax or Finnish noun cases. An elder who learns the intricacies of Korean or Finnish grammar through divinely aided learning might, then, mistake the knowledge he has gained for the gift itself—something firmly in his possession.[10] However, the knowledge he has gained is not the gift but an increased capacity upon which the Lord might draw as necessary. Notwithstanding his knowledge of specific vocabulary or usage rules, that elder's capacity to exercise the gift of tongues is still and always contingent upon the grace of God. The development of a spiritual gift entails both the cultivation of capacity and the receipt of divine power.

Thus, in the Doctrine and Covenants, missionaries are given two potentially competing directives regarding their preaching. In a revelation to Hyrum Smith, the Lord directed this aspiring missionary: "Seek not to declare my word, but first seek to obtain my word, and then shall your tongue be loosed; then, if

---

10 Hugh Nibley suggests that a desire to make the exercise of spiritual gifts reliable, predictable—more like a talent than a manifestation of divine grace—was behind reforms in the early Christian church. Nibley writes that St. Augustine "had learned by hard experience that you can't trust revelation because you can't control it—the Spirit bloweth where *it* listeth, and what the Church needed was something more available and reliable than that." For this reason, Augustine helped shift worship "from Spirit to office, from inspiration to ceremony . . . when the inspired leader was replaced by the typical city bishop, an appointed and elected official. . . . At the same time the charismatic gifts, the spiritual gifts, not to be trusted, were replaced by rites and ceremonies that could be timed and controlled" (Hugh Nibley, "Leaders and Managers" [Brigham Young University commencement, Aug. 19, 1983], speeches. byu.edu).

you desire, you shall have my Spirit and my word, yea, the power of God unto the convincing of men" (D&C 11:21). Obtaining the word, as Hyrum was commanded to do, is a prerequisite to receiving divine assistance and speaking by the gift and power of God to the convincing of others. But merely obtaining the word does not qualify Hyrum or other missionaries to exercise the gift of preaching by the Spirit. In more generalized counsel to early missionaries of the restored Church, Jesus Christ explains that although elders must study to obtain the word, they should not "take . . . thought beforehand what ye shall say; but treasure up in your minds continually the words of life, and it shall be given you in the very hour that portion that shall be meted unto every man" (D&C 84:85). Studying the scriptures and continually treasuring the words of life will cultivate a capacity for the gift of preaching, but the use of that knowledge for the convincing of others must "be given you." In other words, spiritual gifts are not merely aptitudes that can be developed and then demonstrated on command by an individual, like a pianist who sits down at a recital to play a piece she has memorized through dedicated practice. Rather, spiritual gifts are a form of collaboration in which God uses an aptitude we have cultivated or the knowledge we have gained to give peace, assurance, and strength to others who are ready and willing to receive that gift.

Our cultivation of specific skills and knowledge is a necessary but, by itself, insufficient step in the development of a spiritual gift. To return to the previous example, a pianist may be willing and able to play the work of Mozart and other classical composers for an audience, but if her listeners only appreciate jazz, she will be unable to move them. She possesses the capacity to play music, but unless she is given the right music to play, her talent is ineffective and wasted. We must rely upon God, and not merely our talents, in the exercise of spiritual gifts.

A loving Heavenly Father who knows each of us perfectly is, in this analogy, like a composer who has written a piece of music specifically attuned to the individual needs of each listener. Only when the pianist is given *that* piece of music will she be able to use her skill as a gift to communicate God's empathy and love to others. As President Lorenzo Snow testified, "There is a way to reach every human heart."[11] Doing so will require collaboration between disciples who act as God's hands here on earth and the Holy Spirit, which can communicate messages authored for an audience of one through those who, having learned and practiced diligently, are "prepared in all things when I shall send you" (D&C 88:80). Learning and practice are necessary, but because spiritual gifts

---

11 *Teachings of Presidents of the Church: Lorenzo Snow* [2012], 231.

also require the receipt of grace, they cannot be exercised without divine aid. Mormon's inability to preach despite his knowledge and diligent preparation is a reminder that gifts are not talents to be exercised independently by individuals but a collaboration between God and man.

Mormon's experience also warns that the ability to exercise a specific spiritual gift might be lost permanently, for the duration of our mortal lives. Learning to swim or to ride a bicycle creates a form of muscle memory so deeply engrained in our consciousness that its permanence is axiomatic. Something you are sure to remember is "just like riding a bike." But our possession of spiritual gifts is far more tenuous, contingent on our continuing worthiness and, occasionally, on circumstances outside our control—Mormon could not exercise the spiritual gift of preaching because others refused to hear him and not because of any failing on his part. The opportunity to develop and to use certain spiritual gifts is perishable; although God will always receive the repentant sinner with open arms, He has given no assurance that we can, in mortality, be freed from the consequences of our sins or that opportunities squandered will miraculously return to us before death. In the parable of the prodigal son, the sinning, wandering son is received joyfully home by his father, but he is not restored to a fullness of his original inheritance. He receives a robe and a ring, but these gifts are just a fraction of the wealth to which he was originally entitled. So, too, we may be restored through repentance to the use of one or more spiritual gifts while still forfeiting gifts and opportunities that might have been ours if we had refrained from sin and made different choices. Two examples from the Restoration illustrate the contingent and transient nature of some opportunities to exercise spiritual gifts and enjoy their benefits.

When Joseph Smith lent the first manuscript pages of his translation of the Book of Mormon to Martin Harris, he discovered to his great sorrow just how fleeting our grasp on a spiritual gift might be. Because he sinned, fearing man more than God, Joseph was instructed that "although a man may have many revelations, and have power to do many mighty works, yet if he boasts in his own strength, and sets at naught the counsels of God, and follows after the dictates of his own will and carnal desires, he must fall and incur the vengeance of a just God upon him" (D&C 3:4). The Lord warned Joseph that unless he repented, he would "be delivered up and become as other men, and have no more gift" (D&C 3:11). Joseph did repent, and the spiritual gift of translation was "restored unto [him] again," but like the prodigal, he permanently lost a portion of his—and our—inheritance (D&C 10:3). By divine decree, the 116 manuscript pages lost by Harris were never retranslated (see D&C 10:14–46).

Even when repentance allowed Joseph to receive again the spiritual gift he had temporarily lost, there was a real and permanent cost associated with that loss.

Mere months later, Oliver Cowdery learned for himself that opportunities to exercise some spiritual gifts are provisional and fleeting. At the dawn of the Restoration, the Lord instructed Cowdery through the Prophet Joseph Smith that "thou hast a gift. . . . And if thou wilt inquire, thou shalt know mysteries which are great and marvelous; therefore thou shalt exercise thy gift, that thou mayest find out mysteries" (D&C 6:10–11). As an extension of this opportunity to probe behind the veil, Cowdery was offered the opportunity "to translate, even as my servant Joseph" and help bring forth the Book of Mormon (D&C 6:25). However, Cowdery's possession of these gifts was conditional. Even as he was offered an opportunity to inquire and explore "mysteries" and to translate, he was warned, "Make not thy gift known unto any save it be those who are of thy faith. Trifle not with sacred things" (D&C 6:12). By all accounts, Cowdery was circumspect in his communications about the gifts he had been given, and yet, he lost the opportunity to develop the gift of translation within a matter of days. When translation proved difficult, he sought further instruction and was admonished, "without faith you can do nothing; therefore ask in faith. Trifle not with these things" (D&C 8:10). The repetition of that warning— "Trifle not"—suggests the fragility of our hold on spiritual gifts. In subsequent days, the Lord explained to Cowdery that he had lost the gift of translation because "you did not continue as you commenced" and "you took no thought save it was to ask me," therefore "I have taken away this privilege from you" (D&C 9:5, 7). Cowdery's opportunity to translate vanished—permanently.

Too casual in his regard for the gifts of God, Cowdery is a cautionary tale; opportunities to receive or to exercise certain gifts are perishable and must be met with eager, sustained effort, or they will be lost. My oldest son, Gabriel, learned this lesson early in life. Like every small boy, Gabriel wanted a puppy, and at the age of eight, he began to ask regularly for a dog. My wife, Alana, and I already had five small children, and we regarded the prospect of a puppy with some trepidation. But instead of saying no, we established conditions that he would need to meet in order to demonstrate he was responsible enough to receive the desired gift. We told Gabriel that if he wanted a pet, he would have to read the Book of Mormon cover to cover and record his progress and insights in a journal daily. We also informed him that he would need to accomplish another significant goal, presenting him with a range of options from which to choose. He selected one of those options, choosing to work over the course of a summer to skip a grade in math. The terms of our agreement were set—or so we thought. But in the following weeks, two things happened: First, while Gabriel made progress in the scriptures, he read sporadically and at a pace that would lead to him finishing the Book of Mormon in two or three years, far beyond our expected time frame. Second, Gabriel's younger brother David began to ask what *he* would have to do in order to earn a dog. While we were willing to accommodate the desire for a dog, Alana and I knew that bringing multiple dogs into the house would stretch our sanity past the breaking point. So we attached a time limit to Gabriel's goals, informing him that he had to complete his reading of the Book of Mormon and demonstrate his competency in math within a year's time; after that point, his opportunity to earn a dog would expire and pass to David. After we established the perishable nature of our offer to buy him a dog, Gabriel adopted a more regimented reading schedule; the trifling efforts he had made previously blossomed into a sustained course of study, and a year later, he received the promised puppy, which he named Clarence.

We required Gabriel to earn his dog at least in part because we wanted to establish a pattern of daily work whereby he demonstrated his willingness to take responsibility for feeding, exercising with, and cleaning up after Clarence. In other words, our gift would still and always be conditional—not only on his completion of goals established prior to the dog's arrival but on his continuing care for Clarence. When Gabriel complained about taking Clarence for his daily run or collecting his feces from the yard, we cheerfully informed him that we would be happy to find a new home for the dog or transfer its ownership to one of his younger siblings. As soon as he truly understood that we were willing to rescind his gift if he did not care for it appropriately, Gabriel stopped complaining. Our possession and use of spiritual gifts, like Gabriel's ownership of Clarence, is made conditional on our willingness to participate in daily patterns of worship whereby we demonstrate our reverence for and faith in Jesus Christ. Unlike bodily skills, such as swimming or riding a bike, patterns of movement engrained so deeply in our being that they can never be lost, our possession of spiritual gifts is always precarious and provisional. Opportunities to gain or to use a gift may be limited, and the experiences of Joseph Smith, Oliver Cowdery, and Mormon, among whose contemporaries "there were no gifts from the Lord," demonstrate that spiritual gifts can be lost permanently and irrevocably.

Jesus Christ, through whose grace we possess and exercise spiritual gifts, is "the same yesterday, and to day, and for ever" (Hebrews 13:8). Miracles have not ceased because Christ has ascended into heaven or because the day of Pentecost or the Kirtland temple dedication has passed. Rather, "it is by faith that miracles are wrought" and spiritual gifts exercised: "wherefore, if these things have ceased wo be unto the children of men, for it is because of unbelief" (Moroni 7:37). During His mortal ministry, even the Savior of the world was constrained by the unbelief of those with whom He associated. In some places, He could do no mighty work, and on certain occasions—such as when Jesus healed the daughter of Jairus or ascended into the Mount of Transfiguration, for example—he made sure that those who accompanied Him were individuals of faith. The respect of a loving Heavenly Father for our agency means that He allows Himself and His disciples to be constrained by the unbelief of those they associate with; He will force no man to heaven and will force no doubter to witness the miraculous exercise of spiritual gifts. Over the past two centuries, as an increasing portion of the world's population has abandoned their faith in God and adopted a secular worldview, public demonstrations of spiritual gifts have accordingly become more and more rare, not because God or the gifts He gives have changed but because humanity has. And yet, for those with eyes to see and ears to hear, the gifts of God continue to be made manifest in abundance.

CHAPTER 4
DENY NOT THE GIFTS OF GOD

BIBLICAL ACCOUNTS OF JESUS RAISING the daughter of Jairus from the dead highlight the constraints that unbelief imposes on the use and visibility of spiritual gifts. Her healing took place in private, after a jeering multitude had been dismissed, and the biblical narratives suggest that spiritual gifts should not be exercised before a disbelieving public. However, the larger account of this miracle makes it clear that spiritual gifts can be employed appropriately even in the presence of many disbelievers. Although a skeptical public might not recognize their use, evidence of the gifts of God and of dramatic, public, heavenly intervention in human affairs is freely available to those who look for His hand with an eye of faith.

Mark records that as the Master walked with Jairus, "much people followed him, and thronged him" (Mark 5:24). Surrounded by a multitude who wanted to see Him work wonders and heal the daughter of a prominent local leader, Jesus pressed forward through a crowd of curious onlookers, each hoping to see some sign of His great power. Amidst the jostling of many, Jesus stopped abruptly to ask what the Apostles thought a puzzling question: "Who touched my clothes? And his disciples said unto him, Thou seest the multitude thronging thee, and sayest thou, Who touched me?" (Mark 5:30–31). Many had made contact with His clothes or His person, but the Savior knew that one, who "came in the press behind, and touched his garment," had done so intentionally, with a desire to be healed (Mark 5:27). This "certain woman, which had an issue of blood twelve years," had said to herself, "If I may touch but his clothes, I shall be whole" (Mark 5:25, 28). She was correct, and when she had touched the Savior's clothes, "straightway the fountain of her blood was dried up; and she felt in her body that she was healed of that plague" (Mark 5:29). Although she "had suffered many things of many physicians" for more than a decade "and had spent all that she had, and was nothing bettered, but rather grew worse," this certain woman exercised faith in Jesus Christ's ability to heal the affliction which had troubled her for so long (Mark 5:26). Her faith in the Redeemer's healing power was so great that she was made whole without any active participation on His part; Jesus recognized that power or "virtue is gone out of me" only after the fact (Luke 8:46).

The multitude that crowded Jesus as He made His way to the house of Jairus had come to see Him perform a dramatic miracle of healing, but none of those in the crowd—not even His disciples, who walked by His side and believed in His divinity—recognized the significance of this woman's encounter with the Savior. She had exercised a spiritual gift to amazing effect in the middle of a crowded street and in full view of many who were anticipating just such a miracle, yet none but the Master understood what had been done. Many of those who witnessed—or, to be more precise, *failed* to witness—this healing were the very same individuals to whom the Savior would deny entrance when He reached the house of Jairus, the same who "laughed him to scorn" when He declared that the daughter of Jairus "is not dead, but sleepeth" (Luke 8:52). They were, in other words, skeptics of the sort whose unbelief would constrain the Savior on similar occasions and prevent Him from doing some mighty work. This certain woman with an issue of blood had exercised faith to be healed and, by the Savior's grace, worked a mighty miracle in circumstances similar to those which limited Mormon, when he was forbidden to preach and "there were no gifts" (Mormon 1:14–16). Her example provides a model for the exercise and observation of spiritual gifts in the twenty-first century when, because of unbelief, God's power is most commonly administered and made manifest in different and less public ways than in those exceptional cases memorialized in scripture. God suits "his mercies according to the conditions of the children of men" (D&C 46:15) and, recognizing the "different ways that these gifts are administered" (Moroni 10:8), is enabled by the spiritual gift of discernment—a gift that should be eagerly sought after in our day, when the faith of many has grown cold and miracles are wrought in relative anonymity by believers, as by this woman with an issue of blood.

Miracles are brought to pass and spiritual gifts are exercised today by both members of The Church of Jesus Christ of Latter-day Saints and by people of faith and goodwill who are not members of the Church. In a message even more applicable today than when he first delivered it, Nephi taught that Jesus Christ—whose spirit is the power which makes divine gifts operative—"manifesteth himself unto all those who believe in him, by the power of the Holy Ghost;

yea, unto every nation, kindred, tongue, and people, working mighty miracles, signs, and wonders, among the children of men according to their faith" (2 Nephi 26:13). A desire to learn more about spiritual gifts and to recognize God's miracles should lead us to a broad study of individuals who go about doing good, whether they are members of the Church or not.

Consider the example of Derek and Jessica Simmons, whose actions helped to save the lives of nine swimmers and whose story was related by Sister Sharon Eubank of the Relief Society General Presidency. When two young boys were caught in a riptide and pulled out to sea, family members and onlookers attempted to rescue the children only to be caught in the current themselves. Worried that the swimmers might drown before rescue workers could reach them, Derek persuaded more than eighty bystanders to form a human chain stretching from the beach into the ocean, within feet of the struggling swimmers. His wife, Jessica, who is an exceptional swimmer, then helped to ferry the stranded swimmers to the chain and back to the safety of the beach using a boogie board. President Eubank reflected, "Everyone on the beach could think only of traditional solutions, and they were paralyzed. But one couple, in a split second, thought of a different solution. Innovation and creation are spiritual gifts."[1] Although these events were observed by many at the beach and, afterwards, widely reported, President Eubank's is the only account that characterizes Derek and Jessica—who are not members of The Church of Jesus Christ of Latter-day Saints—as the possessors of spiritual gifts. As when Jesus healed the "certain woman" on His way to see the daughter of Jairus, a miracle occurred in plain sight, but only President Eubank, with eyes to see, recognized the role that spiritual gifts played in this rescue and acknowledged that divine virtue, or power, made it possible.

Compare Derek's innovative idea—to form a human chain—with a much more famous seaside rescue, when Jehovah helped the children of Israel cross the Red Sea and find refuge from Pharaoh's army. On that occasion, Moses stood on the beach and listened to the people he had liberated from captivity complain, asking, "wherefore hast thou dealt thus with us, to carry us forth out of Egypt? Is not this the word that we did tell thee in Egypt, saying, Let us alone, that we may serve the Egyptians? For it had been better for us to serve the Egyptians, than that we should die in the wilderness" (Exodus 14:11–12). Jacob's descendants could think only of traditional solutions and, accordingly, assumed that they would die at the hands of Pharaoh's charioteers. But Moses rebuked the people, called on God, and received revelation. Indeed, the Lord instructed Oliver

---

1 Sharon Eubank, "Turn On Your Light," *Ensign* or *Liahona*, Nov. 2017.

Cowdery that this experience is a pattern for those who seek the spiritual gift of revelation, for those who seek innovative and creative solutions to unique and pressing challenges. "Yea, behold," He declared, "I will tell you in your mind and in your heart, by the Holy Ghost, which shall come upon you and which shall dwell in your heart. Now, behold, this is the spirit of revelation; behold, this is the spirit by which Moses brought the children of Israel through the Red Sea on dry ground. Therefore this is thy gift; apply unto it" (D&C 8:2–4).

We recognize that Moses exercised a spiritual gift and received divine aid because of the miraculous manner in which Jehovah delivered His people, but the revelatory insight received by Derek and acted upon by Jessica might seem too minor, too mundane to warrant a comparison with Moses's parting of the Red Sea. Oliver Cowdery felt similarly as he struggled to think of his gift and its exercise as an extension of the powers wielded by Moses. In the absence of a dramatic and public display of divine power, how could he be certain that his own impressions, spoken to his mind and heart by a still, small voice, emanated from the same celestial source?

In addressing this question, Elder Jeffrey R. Holland lamented that we embrace "too narrow a concept of *revelation*"—a critique that might be extended to our similarly narrow conception of many other spiritual gifts.[2] When Moses, standing on the shore of the Red Sea, becomes our standard for the gift of revelation, other communications from heaven might not seem to measure up. But the drama of a sea divided is clearly an atypical occurrence, even in sacred history. On at least two other occasions, prophets brought their people to the seashore, needing to cross a large body of water, and in both cases, rather than parting the waters, the Lord commanded His people to build boats. Nephi was instructed to "construct a ship, after the manner which I shall show thee" (1 Nephi 17:8), but to the brother of Jared, "the Lord said: Go to work and build, after the manner of barges which ye have hitherto built" (Ether 2:16). On these two occasions, as for Moses on the shore of the Red Sea, the gift of revelation facilitated a seaside rescue. Receiving the counsel to build barges "after the manner of barges which ye have hitherto built" might not seem a communication worthy of the word *revelation*, but God will never do for man what man can do for himself. As the poet Dante declared, "The greatest gift that God in His bounty made in creation, the most conformable to His goodness and the one He accounts the most precious, was the freedom of the will," and a loving Father in Heaven will do nothing to diminish the value of

---

2 Jeffrey R. Holland, "Cast Not Away Therefore Your Confidence" [Brigham Young University devotional, Mar. 2, 1999], speeches.byu.edu.

our agency.³ If Moses had arrived on the seashore with the time and timber to construct crafts that could carry his people to safety, surely the spirit of revelation would have brought the children of Israel across the Red Sea in boats and not on dry ground. On the other hand, if Derek and Jessica Simmons had stood on that beach without any resources, it is possible that a merciful Lord would have offered them, as He offered Moses, instructions on how to part the seas, so that the stranded swimmers might walk back to the beach on dry land. However, because Derek and Jessica possessed abundant resources (dozens of compassionate bystanders willing to act) and skills (Jessica's ability to swim through a riptide), the spirit of revelation and innovation instructed them to use their resources and skills on behalf of others. The Simmons acted in public, like the woman with an issue of blood, but because so many embrace a narrow understanding of revelation, only President Eubank recognized that they, like Moses, exercised spiritual gifts to rescue those in need.

In the twenty-first century, as educational opportunities and the proliferation of technology have empowered individuals to act in more effectual ways than ever before, the exercise of spiritual gifts may become increasingly difficult for the unbeliever to recognize. But miracles and gifts continue to abound, and Moroni's warning—"deny not the gifts of God"—was specifically meant for us in latter days (Moroni 10:8). The experiences of a priesthood holder I will call John illustrate some of the challenges associated with recognizing spiritual gifts in a modern context.

John was trained as a dentist in the United States and frequently travels to Central America, where he provides free dental care to individuals who would otherwise have no access to oral medicine. On one occasion, as he and other dentists concluded a clinic held on a mountainside, racing to pack their tools and supplies before a thunderstorm broke above them, a local man in his thirties approached John in obvious pain. An impacted wisdom tooth had become infected and needed to be pulled, but John and his colleagues could not remove the tooth; they lacked the training and tools—such as an X-ray machine—to operate effectively in this particular circumstance. They attempted to pull the

---

3 Dante, *The Divine Comedy*, trans. John D. Sinclair, vol. 3, *Paradiso* (New York: Oxford University Press, 1939), 75. Elder David A. Bednar has taught this principle repeatedly, urging members of the Church to "pray for the strength to learn from, change, or accept our circumstances rather than praying relentlessly for God to change our circumstances according to our will. We will become agents who act rather than objects that are acted upon" (David A. Bednar, "Bear Up Their Burdens with Ease," *Ensign* or *Liahona*, May 2014).

tooth repeatedly, using several different tools and techniques, but to no avail. Knowing that he was the man's only hope of relief, John offered a silent prayer for direction. In response, he received a clear impression directing him to open a flap of gum tissue, exposing the man's jaw and impacted tooth from a new angle. After cutting this flap, "not knowing beforehand the things which [he] should do," a second impression followed, directing John to pick up a specific dental tool—an elevator, used to pry teeth from their sockets—and to insert it backwards, at an angle and in a way that he had never before seen this tool used (1 Nephi 4:6). As he followed these promptings, the tooth, which had resisted the pull of extracting forceps, immediately sprang out of the man's mouth. At this point, John explained, the step-by-step instruction of the Spirit ceased, and he was left with one final prompting, directing him to use his training and expertise to staunch the bleeding and care for the new wound in this man's mouth. Drawing on both the direction of the Spirit and the education he had received, John removed the tooth and relieved the pain of his patient by performing a procedure he had never before seen, using a tool with which he was familiar in a novel way. He had exercised the gift of healing.

When I approached John some weeks after he first shared this story in a sacrament meeting talk, to ask if I might include it in this book as an example of the gift of healing, he regarded me with concern. "Did I say that I had the gift of healing in my talk?" he asked. "The early Christians," Hugh Nibley once observed, "called *Christemporoi* [or Christ-peddlers] those who made merchandise of spiritual gifts," but John had not spoken of this experience lightly or used the language of spiritual gifts as an ecclesiastical status symbol.[4] During our ensuing, private discussion about the sacred nature of his experience on that mountainside, John confided to me that his patriarchal blessing did indeed identify him as one who possessed "faith to heal" (D&C 46:20). As a dentist, he explained, he offered silent prayers each day while working on the mouths of his patients. In many cases, these prayers expressed only gratitude for the ability to recognize his patients' needs and to treat them effectively. On rarer occasions, when confronted with a difficult procedure, he offered prayers requesting guidance so that he could operate successfully and restore his patients

---

4 Hugh Nibley, "Leaders and Managers" [Brigham Young University commencement, Aug. 19, 1983], speeches.byu.edu. As Elder James A. Cullimore warned, "It was not intended that we make merchandise out of the gifts of God and shout to the world the result of these most wonderful gifts. They are given to us for our salvation, to strengthen our testimony and the testimonies of others as we bear humble witness of them in our meetings, quietly, by the Spirit but not before the world" (James A. Cullimore, "Gifts of the Spirit," *Ensign*, Nov. 1974).

to good health. Although he drew on both his formal training and on his faith to heal daily, neither his patients nor the members of his staff had ever recognized that he possessed and exercised the spiritual gift of healing. John drew on the powers of heaven in a public space and at times exercised his gift on behalf of unbelievers, but as in the case of the woman with an issue of blood, few or none of those observing recognized the miracles he performed in their presence.

Miracles may look different and may be more subtle in our day, when the Lord uses the increased capacity of His children to effect changes that would have required more dramatic solutions in previous dispensations, but He also continues to work in much the same manner that He always has. As I queried John about his experiences with the gift of healing, he shared several stories that might be more in keeping with a narrow or traditional view of that power. On one of his trips to Central America, a local bishop explained that he needed surgery to insert a stent that would relieve pressure in his kidneys. The bishop had felt prompted to wait until John and the other American dentists with whom he traveled had arrived before asking for a blessing of healing and undergoing the surgery. Although John was one of several priesthood holders present, several of whom held more prominent positions in the Church and might, therefore, have seemed like more natural choices, the bishop asked him to speak as voice during the blessing. During the ordinance, John—who learned Spanish on these trips and was never taught the language in a formal setting—found himself using medical terminology and grammatical constructions that he had never learned and with which he was unfamiliar. On this occasion, his spiritual gift of healing was made manifest in a priesthood ordinance.

A similar manifestation occurred on another occasion, when John was visiting the newborn intensive care unit of a hospital, where one of John's friends was observing his fragile, dramatically premature children struggle for survival. The newborn babies had arrived so early that doctors feared for their survival; when John was asked to offer the babies a priesthood blessing, he felt inspired to promise that each would live, thrive, and lead a normal, healthy life—which they have, despite the dire outlook when he administered to them. Although those healed by his faith may not always be aware that John is exercising a spiritual gift, John's gift of healing has facilitated his public, professional work as a dentist both on Central American mountainsides and in his own office as well as in more traditional settings as he has administered priesthood blessings to the sick and suffering.

John's use of dental training to heal may not fit with our expectations of spiritual gifts, but God rarely, if ever, intervenes in human affairs until and unless His children have first exhausted their own resources. Faith to heal is often accompanied by promptings to provide innovative medical care, as the Lord draws on available knowledge and medical technology, in addition to faith, while healing the afflicted. In biblical times, for example, when Elisha was called to the home of a Shunammite woman whose only son had died, he physically administered to the boy: "And he went up, and lay upon the child, and put his mouth upon his mouth, and his eyes upon his eyes, and his hands upon his hands: and he stretched himself upon the child; and the flesh of the child waxed warm" (2 Kings 4:34). While the operative power in this miracle may have been Elisha's priesthood authority, after he "prayed unto the Lord," Elisha felt inspired to place his mouth over the boy's and breathe into it in a manner reminiscent of modern medical practice (2 Kings 4:33). In this case, the spiritual gift of faith to heal was augmented by the administration of something like cardiopulmonary resuscitation—long before that technique was pioneered in the nineteenth century. Although we may recognize the means by which Elisha healed the boy, his healing is no less miraculous than if Elisha had simply commanded him to live.

Before his call as an Apostle, President Russell M. Nelson worked for many years as a heart surgeon and pioneered many new surgical techniques. On one occasion, Dr. Nelson recounted, a man from southern Utah, whose defective tricuspid valve made him a poor candidate for surgery, persuaded him to operate despite his

> not knowing exactly the technique required. The operation had not been done before. I operated upon him, and, in the middle of the operation, I had the most wonderful vision of what should be done—dotted lines as to where the stitches should be laid. I opened his heart up and placed the stitches right where I saw them in that diagram that flashed before my mind, and the operation worked beautifully.[5]

This revelatory experience, which provided President Nelson an understanding of how best to operate on his patient's heart, is similar to that received by my friend John on a Central American mountainside. In both cases, prayers offered by trained medical professionals were answered with divine inspiration detailing new surgical techniques; in both cases, faith to heal supplemented and augmented the technical skills already possessed by a trained healer.

These moments of individual ministration, during which a single, inspired doctor operates with divine aid on a single, problematic patient, likely fit our

---

5 As quoted in Spencer J. Condie, *Russell M. Nelson: Father, Surgeon, Apostle* (Salt Lake City, UT: Deseret Book, 2003), 151.

paradigm for the exercise of spiritual gifts. But what of other moments in the career of President Nelson, such as when he collaborated with his wife and other medical professionals to develop new medical technologies that would be used to save the lives of many? During the 1950s, Dr. Nelson and his wife, Dantzel, worked together to construct a machine that would first oxygenate the blood of patients undergoing open-heart surgery and then return the oxygenated blood to a patient's body without any foam or air bubbles. Like Derek and Jessica Simmons, they labored together, drawing on complementary skill sets to create an innovative new pump-oxygenator. After Dr. Nelson explained the technical challenges of aerating and then defoaming his patients' blood, he and Dantzel "snipped off the closed-end of a rubber nursing nipple that we had used to feed our babies. To that opening we tied an oxygen line. To the larger open end of the nursing nipple we glued a rubber diaphragm, which Dantzel had perforated about a hundred times with tiny pricks of her sewing machine needle."[6] This prototype became the basis for a pump-oxygenator that would be used first by Dr. Nelson and then by his colleagues, allowing surgeons in Utah and elsewhere to operate more successfully on patients needing open-heart procedures. The same spiritual gifts of innovation and healing which allowed Dr. Nelson to operate on a defective tricuspid valve are evident in his collaborative efforts to develop a new pump-oxygenator, but few would recognize this widely publicized development in thoracic medicine as a comparable miracle or the product of spiritual gifts. Because the means by which Dr. Nelson and Dantzel developed this new machine are better understood than the means by which Moses parted the Red Sea or the means by which priesthood blessings of healing preserve and improve the health of recipients, they are also more easily dismissed as mere human contributions to our health and well-being.

Spiritual gifts and miracles abound in our day, as in Elisha's, but the ability of experts to identify the means by which they are exercised may prevent us from recognizing their divine origins. In the New Testament, when Peter and John were brought before the high priest, elders, and scribes to "be examined of the good deed done to the impotent man, by what means he is made whole," they declared that they had effected his healing "by the name of Jesus Christ of Nazareth" (Acts 4:9–10). Those who exercise spiritual gifts in the twenty-first century might make the same declaration, even when the processes by which those gifts impact others are readily explicable to lay persons, as in the case of medical professionals who develop new surgical techniques or use extant medical technologies in new and innovative ways. Alma explains in the Book

---

6 Condie, *Russell M. Nelson: Father, Surgeon, Apostle*, 130.

of Mormon that "the Lord God doth work by means to bring about his great and eternal purposes," and the fact that we can identify those means, or the secondary causes by which He works, offers no reason to doubt that He is ultimately responsible for their use (Alma 37:7). No one who sees a beautiful work of art attributes all credit to the paintbrush, even if it is the immediate cause by which oils were transformed into a masterpiece; neither should we ignore or fail to acknowledge the hand of the Lord when He works through secondary causes which we can understand.

The spiritual gift of innovation manifest in the work of Dr. Nelson is also evident in the emergence of other medical, communication, transportation, and manufacturing technologies developed by individuals who belong to different faiths. For example, consider the Karnaphuli Paper Mills, built in the mid-twentieth century to process bamboo into paper. Shortly after the mill's opening, the bamboo forests it was to exploit died, leaving its operators without raw materials for the mills. Malcolm Gladwell writes that in response,

> the mill's operators quickly found ways to bring in bamboo from villages throughout East Pakistan, building a new supply chain using the country's many waterways. They started a research program to find faster-growing species of bamboo to replace the dead forests, and planted an experimental tract. They found other kinds of lumber that worked just as well. The result was that the plant was blessed with a far more diversified base of raw materials than had ever been imagined. If bad planning hadn't led to the crisis at the Karnaphuli plant, the mill's operators would never have been forced to be creative.

When the economist Albert Hirschman considered the Karnaphuli Paper Mills and the innovative solutions that preserved them from ruin, he concluded that "We may be dealing here with a general principle of action. . . . Creativity always comes as a surprise to us; therefore we can never count on it and we dare not believe in it until it has happened. In other words, we would not consciously engage upon tasks whose success clearly requires that creativity be forthcoming."[7] Moses might not have led the children of Israel out of Egypt if he had known that they would have to cross the Red Sea so quickly, without boats. My friend John might not have begun operating on that Central American mountainside if he had known that traditional operating methods would fail. Creativity comes

---

7 As quoted in Malcolm Gladwell, "The Gift of Doubt," *The New Yorker*, June 17, 2013, https://www.newyorker.com/magazine/2013/06/24/the-gift-of-doubt.

as a surprise because it is a spiritual gift given by God to His children around the world when they seek to do good and confront unexpected challenges. Those with eyes to see will recognize these gifts and what Hirschman called "the hiding hand" that makes them available.

Exercised in our midst on a regular basis, spiritual gifts bless all facets of our lives. As Elder Dallin H. Oaks once testified to Church Educational System teachers, "many miracles happen every day in the work of our Church and in the lives of our members. Many of you have witnessed miracles, perhaps more than you realize."[8] Some of these miracles are a product of spiritual gifts, as God's children exercise exceedingly great faith and receive, as a result, the power to heal others, to speak in tongues or interpret tongues, to still a storm, and to raise the dead.

At times, as when the Savior healed the daughter of Jairus, the Spirit constrains those with faith to exercise spiritual gifts and work miracles, directing them to wait until unbelievers have departed before proceeding. Such was the case in Tonga when a three-year-old girl died after being run over by a taxi, leaving her head crushed and her face disfigured. When her father prepared to administer a priesthood blessing, he received "the distinct impression that I should not continue with the ordinance. It was as if a voice were speaking to me saying: 'This is not the right time, for the place is full of mockers and unbelievers. Wait for a more private moment.'" Only hours later, in the privacy of their home, did the father feel able to administer to the lifeless body of his daughter, asking God "to open the doors of Paradise, so I could tell her to come back and receive her body again and live." Miraculously, this young woman, whose dead body had been observed by many, rose from her bed hale, whole, and alive. Her wounds had been healed, and her spirit had returned.[9] If such accounts are rare, it is at least in part because God warns "that they shall not boast themselves of these things, neither speak them before the world" (D&C 84:73).

In contrast to this miraculous healing which, like that of the daughter of Jairus, could take place only in an atmosphere of privacy and faith, Elder Oaks recounts another modern miracle which was widely observed and yet not necessarily recognized by those observing as an occasion on which divine power was manifest. In 1989, military leaders attempted to overthrow the government of Philippine President Corazon Aquino, and combat ensued in the vicinity of

---

8 Dallin H. Oaks, "Miracles" (from a talk given at a Church Educational System fireside in Calgary, Alberta, Canada, on 7 May 2000), *Ensign*, June 2001.

9 Eric B. Shumway, *Tongan Saints: Legacy of Faith* (Laie, HI: Institute for Polynesian Studies, 1998), 88–89.

the Manila Philippines Temple. Rebel soldiers occupied the temple grounds and exchanged fire with government troops: a government helicopter strafed the temple grounds before being driven off by rebel machine guns, and a government plane dropped several bombs that hit the temple patron residence (then under construction) near the temple. The temple grounds eventually became the last remaining rebel stronghold in Manila, and government forces gathered artillery and troops for a devastating assault. In a remarkable coincidence, the First Presidency and Quorum of the Twelve had, weeks earlier, scheduled an unusual Sunday morning meeting that was to begin at the very hour that government forces had designated for their assault on the temple grounds.[10] As the Prophet and assembled Apostles pleaded with the Lord to protect His house, rebel soldiers abandoned the temple grounds, and the government assault was canceled. After the conflict was over, retired military personnel who inspected temple grounds concluded that six mortar or rocket shells had exploded on temple grounds and that, based on their trajectory, "some of these shells had to have passed between the spires of the temple." Notwithstanding gunfire and bombing that impacted adjacent church structures, the temple itself was marked by only "one bullet hole, apparently a single stray rifle shot, at the top of the highest steeple." In his personal journal, Elder Oaks described the temple's preservation as "a miracle of divine intervention no less impressive than many recorded in holy writ," and local Church officials declared that "an unseen army of angels assisted faithful temple guards that the temple was not desecrated."[11] Although the mortal soldiers in attendance may not have seen these heavenly guardians, their influence on this public event was plainly evident to those with eyes to see.

This miracle was accomplished in public, yet most of those who were eyewitnesses to its accomplishment lacked the faith necessary to see God's hand working to preserve the temple in response to the prayers of His Apostles. However, when the faithful gather together, spiritual gifts may still be exercised and observed publicly in our day, with dramatic effects witnessed by all who are present—as in the days of Pentecost, Kirtland, and Nauvoo. Speaking in general conference as a member of the Quorum of the Twelve Apostles, Elder Nelson recounted

---

10 Speaking of the word *coincidence*, Elder Neal A. Maxwell declared, "This word is understandable for mortals to use, but *coincidence* is not an appropriate word to describe the workings of an omniscient God. He does not do things by 'coincidence' but . . . by 'divine design'" ("Brim with Joy" [Brigham Young University devotional, Jan. 23, 1996], speeches.byu.edu). See also Ronald A. Rasband, "By Divine Design," *Ensign* or *Liahona*, Nov. 2017.

11 Oaks, "Miracles."

witnessing such a miracle while traveling to New Zealand with President Spencer W. Kimball many years earlier.

President Kimball was scheduled to address a large gathering of youth, but he and his wife, Camilla, fell ill. Stricken with high fevers, each was given a priesthood blessing and then laid down to rest, resigned to missing the cultural celebration prepared by the youth. Elder Nelson remained with President Kimball and Camilla, who were sleeping, while Sister Nelson and President N. Eldon Tanner left to attend the celebration. Elder Nelson recalled,

> While President Kimball was sleeping, I was quietly reading in his room. Suddenly President Kimball was awakened. He asked, "Brother Nelson, what time was this evening's program to begin?"
>
> "At seven o'clock, President Kimball."
>
> "What time is it now?"
>
> "It's almost seven," I replied.
>
> President Kimball quickly said, "Tell Sister Kimball we are going!"
>
> I checked President Kimball's temperature. It was normal! I took Sister Kimball's temperature. It was also normal!
>
> They quickly dressed and got into an automobile. We were driven to the stadium of the Church College of New Zealand. As the car entered the arena, there was a very loud shout that erupted spontaneously. It was most unusual! After we took our seats, I asked Sister Nelson about that sudden sound. She said that when President Tanner began the meeting, he dutifully excused President and Sister Kimball because of illness. Then one of the young New Zealanders was called upon to pray.
>
> With great faith, he gave what Sister Nelson described as a rather lengthy but powerful prayer. He so prayed: "We are 3,000 New Zealand youth. We are assembled here, having prepared for six months to sing and dance for Thy prophet. Wilt Thou heal him and deliver him here!" After the "amen" was pronounced, the car carrying President and Sister Kimball entered the stadium. They were identified immediately, and instantly everyone shouted for joy![12]

---

12 Russell M. Nelson, "Jesus Christ—the Master Healer," *Ensign* or *Liahona*, Nov. 2005.

The faith to heal, which was evident in the prayer of this New Zealand youth, brought about an immediate and marvelous response that was witnessed by thousands. President Kimball's timely and dramatic recovery provides evidence that spiritual gifts may still be exercised publicly and miraculously in our day, wherever the faithful gather.[13]

The number of miracles experienced and spiritual gifts exercised by our family members, friends, and acquaintances exceeds our present knowledge. In part, our ignorance results from failing to recognize God's hand and then crediting the means by which these miracles and gifts were accomplished rather than the Creator of those means. But our relative ignorance of such moments and capacities is also, in part, a function of the Messianic meekness that is a prerequisite for the exercise of spiritual gifts.[14] Those who consistently draw on the powers of heaven treat their experiences of spiritual gifts as sacred, sharing their specific knowledge of the miraculous goodness of God only when authorized by the Spirit. To wit: over the last thirty years, I have heard my mother, Priscilla Glass Hutchins, relate the story of her conversion to the gospel of Jesus Christ dozens of times. So I was shocked when, in a recent private conversation about spiritual matters, she shared additional details about her conversion and subsequent life of discipleship that identified her as the possessor of a spiritual gift I had never imagined her to possess. The special experiences she described to me were pivotal in her decision to live a life of faith, but even fifty years after they had taken place, she was reluctant to share them unless specifically prompted to do so by the Holy Ghost. Those who treat spiritual gifts as a form of ecclesiastical currency will soon find themselves bankrupt, but to those who seek in humility, and not for a sign, evidences of the reality of spiritual gifts invariably appear.

As individuals of faith search for evidence of miracles and spiritual gifts, the influence of angels and the exercise of divine power will be made manifest.

---

13 Gatherings of the faithful where spiritual gifts might be exercised include gatherings in which few or none of the participants may be members of our faith. To wit, Elder Oaks describes just such "a miracle. When a five-year-old girl breathed with difficulty and became feverish, her parents rushed her to the hospital. By the time she arrived there, her kidneys and lungs had shut down, her fever was 107 degrees, and her body was bright red and covered with purple lesions. The doctors said she was dying of toxic shock syndrome, cause unknown. As word spread to family and friends, God-fearing people began praying for her, and a special prayer service was held in their Protestant congregation in Waco, Texas. Miraculously, she suddenly returned from the brink of death and was released from the hospital in a little over a week" ("Healing the Sick," *Ensign* or *Liahona*, May 2010).

14 See David A. Bednar, "Meek and Lowly of Heart," *Ensign* or *Liahona*, May 2018.

Indeed, we will experience the wonder of Elisha's servant when an army surrounded the city in which they resided; he cried out, "Alas, my master! how shall we do?" Elisha responded, "Fear not: for they that be with us are more than they that be with them. And Elisha prayed, and said, Lord, I pray thee, open his eyes, that he may see. And the Lord opened the eyes of the young man; and he saw: and, behold, the mountain was full of horses and chariots of fire round about Elisha" (2 Kings 6:15–17). In this day, as in prior ages, "to some is given the working of miracles," and many exercise spiritual gifts in our midst (D&C 46:21). Even when those miracles and gifts are performed or exercised publicly, we may discount or fail to recognize them because we are focused on the means or immediate causes by which they bless our lives and the lives of others. But it is "by small means" that the Lord most frequently works to "bring about great things" (1 Nephi 16:29); rather than working *ex nihilo*, God generally provides "a means that man, through faith, might work mighty miracles" (Mosiah 8:18). In the hustle and bustle of the crowd, as we metaphorically press forward to the house of Jairus in search of some great sign, we may miss the miracles in our midst unless we are willing to see that a seemingly mundane gesture—one hand among many, touching the Savior's robes—can be the means of exercising a spiritual gift and drawing down the powers, or virtue, of heaven.

PART TWO

Case Studies from the Book of Mormon

Latter-day Saints who have faith in the continuing efficacy of spiritual gifts and who understand the purposes for which they are given will naturally desire to develop additional gifts, beyond those which they already possess. This desire to call down the powers of heaven will most readily be accomplished as Saints immerse themselves in the Book of Mormon, which was prepared as a spiritual guide for the challenges and opportunities specific to our day. As others have noted, Lehi's descendants never possessed this volume of scripture. We are its intended—its only—audience, and the Book of Mormon is the appointed means by which we are to draw closer to a loving Father in Heaven during this dispensation. Thus, Joseph Smith "told the brethren that the Book of Mormon was the most correct of any book on earth, and the keystone of our religion, and a man would get nearer to God by abiding by its precepts, than by any other book."[1] In addition to its plain and precious teachings on many other subjects, the Book of Mormon regularly reminds readers of the need to seek for spiritual gifts and offers counsel on how we can qualify to receive these gifts. It is the keystone in our quest to become more like God, and we will receive His gifts more readily by studying its pages and applying its precepts than by any other means.

The very title page of the Book of Mormon foregrounds the role that spiritual gifts played in its preparation, preservation, discovery, translation, and publication. Moroni writes, on the title page, that the records included in the Book of Mormon were "Written and sealed up, and hid up unto the Lord, that they might not be destroyed—To come forth by the gift and power of God unto the interpretation thereof—Sealed by the hand of Moroni, and hid up unto the Lord, to come forth in due time by way of the Gentile—The interpretation thereof by the gift of God." Reading Moroni's words and the sacred narrative

---

1 *Teachings of Presidents of the Church: Joseph Smith* [2007], 64.

which follows should cause us to reflect on the various spiritual gifts involved in the creation of the Book of Mormon. Some are obvious. Moroni highlights the gift of preaching, noting that the powerful sermons recorded in this volume of scripture were delivered only because "thou hast made all this people that they could speak much" and "made us mighty in word" (Ether 12:23). Mormon could have ended his record after abridging all of Nephite history, but instead, he "searched among the records which had been delivered into my hands" and found the small plates of Nephi, which comprise the first third of the published record; his spiritual gift of searching is both a reason we have the Book of Mormon and a model for our own study of its teachings (Words of Mormon 1:3). And, of course, the gift of visions was obviously instrumental both in Lehi's escape from Jerusalem and in Joseph Smith's ability to locate the plates. The gifts of preaching, searching, and receiving visions played clear and obvious roles in the preparation of the Book of Mormon. But so, too, did more subtle gifts, including the gift of believing on the words of others (see Mosiah 17:2–4) and the gift of mighty prayer (see Enos 1:13). Moroni's title page encourages us to acknowledge and enumerate the spiritual gifts exercised by the men and women of the Book of Mormon; it also reminds us that our interpretations of scripture must come "by the gift of God."

Elder David A. Bednar has provided a pattern for studying both the Book of Mormon and spiritual gifts in the manner suggested by Moroni. For example, reading Mormon's sermon on faith, hope, and charity in Moroni 7:42–44 led Elder Bednar to identify "meekness as the foundation from which all spiritual capacities and gifts arise".[2] This insight provides essential guidance to all who would "seek . . . earnestly the best gifts," suggesting that the first spiritual gift for which we should seek is the meekness and lowliness of heart exemplified by the Savior; without meekness, we cannot hope to qualify for the other spiritual gifts we desire (D&C 46:8). Studying the Book of Mormon provides us models of meekness tailored to the particular challenges of our day, including Amulek, who forsook wealth and popularity to preach the word, and Pahoran, who responded to the unjust accusations of Captain Moroni with patience and forgiveness.

In the same way that a study of the words and deeds of Amulek and Pahoran will provide us with a greater understanding of meekness, a study of the lives of other ancient American disciples will teach us how to identify and develop each of the spiritual gifts to which we might appropriately aspire. Here, too, Elder Bednar has shown the way. In a devotional address at Brigham Young University, he spoke about the life of Mormon in order to emphasize the importance of an

---

2 David A. Bednar, "Meek and Lowly of Heart," *Ensign* or *Liahona*, May 2018.

"underappreciated spiritual gift—the capacity of being 'quick to observe.'" Elder Bednar then offered additional examples of this gift and its many applications in modern life, drawing connections between Mormon's gift and "the world in which we do now and will yet live."[3] As we prayerfully study the lives of Amulek, Pahoran, Mormon, and others, we will recognize numerous desirable gifts and be taught how best to "liken all scriptures unto us, that it might be for our profit and learning" (1 Nephi 19:23). Studying the Book of Mormon in this manner is the best way to learn about and qualify to receive the spiritual gifts with which God desires to bless us.

Accordingly, the following four chapters provide a template for this method of study. Each considers a single divine aptitude whose development and use is evident in the life of a figure from the Book of Mormon. Every chapter begins with a close reading of that gift's manifestation in the Book of Mormon before shifting to modern exemplars who have exercised the gift in contemporary circumstances. These case studies, which present familiar figures through a unique lens by identifying the spiritual gifts that allowed them to be successful in their ministries, demonstrate the breadth of gifts available to God's children and show how our study of the Book of Mormon might facilitate the recognition and development of spiritual gifts. Chapter five considers Lehi and the gift of gratitude; chapter six, Abish and the gift of gathering; chapter seven, Teancum and the gift of being anxiously engaged; chapter eight, Nephi, son of Helaman, and the gift of unwearyingness. These chapters on the keystone of our religion provide a pattern for identifying and developing spiritual gifts by introducing readers to gifts seldom discussed over the pulpit and modeling methods of scripture study that will facilitate a pursuit of new spiritual capacities.

---

3 David A. Bednar, "Quick to Observe" [Brigham Young University devotional, May 10, 2005], speeches.byu.edu.

CHAPTER 5
LEHI AND THE GIFT OF GRATITUDE

As a prophet called to warn the people of Jerusalem and to lead a small group of the faithful into exile, Lehi necessarily possessed a wide range of spiritual gifts. He was one to whom "it may be given to have all those gifts, that there may be a head" (D&C 46:29). Nephi's first words in the Book of Mormon attest to his father's facility with tongues and their interpretation, and Lehi's prophesying famously drew the ire of Jerusalem's inhabitants, who sought to slay him rather than listen to his declarations that the city would soon be destroyed. Like his ancestor, Joseph of Egypt, Lehi also possessed the gift of dreams and the interpretation of dreams; his vision of the tree of life and his explanation of that vision's symbols is one of the most precious and frequently read passages in the Book of Mormon. Lehi was clearly a man of many gifts, some of which were spectacular in nature, and yet the aptitude most abundantly manifest in Nephi's account of his life and teachings is a more subtle endowment: the spiritual gift of gratitude.

Nephi's narrative begins with the news that Jerusalem is to be razed and many of its inhabitants carried into Babylon. While out walking, Lehi pauses to pray and is surprised to find a pillar of fire upon a rock before him, through which he receives instructions from God. He returns home and throws himself onto his bed, only to be "carried away in a vision," in which he learns that Jerusalem will be devastated by the sword and that many of those who survive will be taken into captivity (1 Nephi 1:8). In response to this news—that the city in which he lives will be destroyed, most of its residents slaughtered, and many of the survivors enslaved—Lehi reacts with what can only be described as a surprising spirit of gratitude. He responds with praise and rejoicing, exclaiming, "Great and marvelous are thy works, O Lord God Almighty! Thy throne is high in the heavens, and thy power, and goodness, and mercy are over all the inhabitants of the earth; and, because thou art merciful, thou wilt not suffer those who come unto thee that they shall perish!" (1 Nephi 1:14). This expression of thanks is Lehi's first recorded speech act, and its grateful tone is characteristic of his words and deeds throughout the Book of Mormon.

When, for example, Lehi is commanded to flee Jerusalem, abandoning his ancestral homeland and all his worldly possessions without any mention, as yet, of a promised land, his first act after leaving the city is to give a material expression of his gratitude. After enduring the scorn and assassination attempts of those condemned by his prophetic message, Lehi leaves his home, taking "nothing with him, save it were his family, and provisions, and tents, and departed into the wilderness" (1 Nephi 2:4). He travels for three days before establishing a semi-permanent camp, and his first concern in this new, desert home is to offer sacrifice: "he built an altar of stones, and made an offering unto the Lord, and gave thanks unto the Lord our God" (1 Nephi 2:7). Thank offerings, as described in the Old Testament, were voluntary sacrifices offered at the discretion of an individual who wished to express that he or she was at peace with God; there was no schedule or calendar necessitating this form of sacrifice. Further, this expression of gratitude required significant labor and came at a cost. Before he could make his thank offering, Lehi had to build an altar of stones— backbreaking work that he begins spontaneously, voluntarily after three days of difficult travel. And then, once the altar is constructed, he kills an animal, which represents his future food supply, the "provisions" he has brought on this journey, as an expression of gratitude. All that Lehi says and does in these opening chapters of the Book of Mormon evinces a spirit of gratitude, even when it might seem that he has little for which to be grateful.

Compare Lehi's actions, in offering sacrifice, to a scene that regularly plays itself out in the lives of Church members. As a youth, I noticed that whenever members of the Church began a significant journey, whether by car or, occasionally, on foot, they would start these trips with a special prayer, petitioning the Lord for safety in their travels. For the most part, these trips were not especially dangerous or taxing; modern travel allows passengers to sit in an automobile or airplane and to pass the time spent traveling in pleasant diversions. Even when travel requires some form of physical exertion, as participants hike, bike, or row a boat, we generally regard this exercise as a recreational experience rather than a necessity. Prayers for a safe journey are ubiquitous, and yet I have observed that when travelers reach their destination without harm or accident, as requested, they rarely express gratitude for the realization of their desires. Disposed to "thank the Lord thy God in all things," Lehi consistently counted his blessings, even when it might have appeared that there were few reasons to give thanks (D&C 59:7).

While we can cultivate the spiritual gift of gratitude in any circumstances and should, perhaps, devote greater energies to its development in times of prosperity than in periods of need, those whose lives most clearly exemplify this gift are often individuals who have experienced tragedy or who struggle with significant challenges. Like Lehi, those whose lives epitomize the spiritual gift of gratitude are generally observed giving thanks in the midst of their trials, not celebrating their absence. When we see such individuals feel, express, and demonstrate gratitude despite their sorrows or hardships, we recognize more clearly the need to give thanks for our comparatively easy and prosperous lives. In His sermon on the mount, Jesus upended traditional wisdom about who, in our lives, deserves love and honor:

> Ye have heard that it hath been said, Thou shalt love thy neighbour, and hate thine enemy. But I say unto you, Love your enemies, bless them that curse you, do good to them that hate you, and pray for them which despitefully use you, and persecute you; that ye may be the children of your Father which is in heaven: for he maketh his sun to rise on the evil and on the good, and sendeth rain on the just and on the unjust. For if ye love them which love you, what reward have ye? do not even the publicans the same? (Matthew 5:43–46)

Similar logic applies in our efforts to feel, express, and demonstrate gratitude. If we only give thanks for unambiguous blessings received during the successful interludes of our lives, why should we expect a reward or think of ourselves as demonstrating true gratitude? Even the least grateful among us might be expected to give thanks in such circumstances. Just as the truly charitable pray for and show kindness to their enemies, those with the gift of gratitude offer thanks in times of trial and temptation as well as in periods of prosperity.

When President Thomas S. Monson taught about our need to develop the spiritual gift of gratitude, he shared the experiences of a Polynesian man named Meli Mulipola, who had been struck blind. President Monson related,

> His vision had been normal until that fateful day when, while working on a pineapple plantation, light turned suddenly to darkness and day became perpetual night. He had learned of the restoration of the gospel and the teachings of The Church of Jesus Christ of Latter-day Saints. His life had been brought into compliance with these teachings.

He and his loved ones had made this long voyage, having learned that one who held the priesthood of God was visiting among the islands. He sought a blessing under the hands of those who held the sacred priesthood. His wish was granted. Tears streamed from his sightless eyes and coursed down his brown cheeks, tumbling finally upon his native dress. He dropped to his knees and prayed: "Oh, God, thou knowest I am blind. Thy servants have blessed me that if it be thy will, my sight may return. Whether in thy wisdom I see light or whether I see darkness all the days of my life, I will be eternally grateful for the truth of thy gospel which I now see and which provides me the light of life."[1]

This man, President Monson taught, exemplified the gift of gratitude, giving thanks unconditionally and in the midst of his trials. Brother Mulipola's gratitude for the gospel and the laying on of hands was not contingent on the restoration of his sight; rather, he offered thanks for compensatory blessings with the recognition that his circumstances might never change. This willingness to reorient his thoughts, directing attention toward the tender mercies already manifest in his life and away from a desire for more, different, or better opportunities is fundamental to the development of gratitude.

Readers of the Book of Mormon frequently contrast the murmuring of Laman and Lemuel with the steadfast faith of Nephi but seldom speak of Lehi's role in modeling an attitude of belief and thanksgiving for his youngest son. In his second general conference address after being ordained an Apostle, Elder David A. Bednar memorably directed the attention of Church members to an expression of gratitude made by Nephi. After recounting the persecution suffered by his father, Nephi declared that he would "show unto you that the tender mercies of the Lord are over all those whom he hath chosen" (1 Nephi 1:20). Elder Bednar explained that these "tender mercies are the very personal and individualized blessings, strength, protection, assurances, guidance, loving-kindnesses, consolation, support, and spiritual gifts which we receive from and because of and through the Lord Jesus Christ." To recognize such blessings in our lives, he continued, is to have our hearts "filled with gratitude for His abundant and tender mercies."[2] Nephi's capacity to discern and to feel gratitude for the tender mercies of the Lord is, in large part, what differentiates him from his

---

1 Thomas S. Monson, "For I Was Blind, but Now I See," *Ensign*, May 1999.
2 David A. Bednar, "The Tender Mercies of the Lord," *Ensign* or *Liahona*, May 2005.

murmuring older brothers. When he speaks to Laman and Lemuel, Nephi constantly reminds them of God's goodness to those who keep covenant; attempting to help his brothers recognize the Lord's tender mercies to past exiles, he cites Moses's deliverance from the armies of Pharaoh on three different occasions as a stimulus to faith and thanksgiving in their present circumstances (see 1 Nephi 4:1–2; 17:25–35; 22:17–20). Nephi's ability to identify the Lord's tender mercies and his willingness to give thanks for God's divine direction of human affairs enables him to exercise the faith for which he is famous—going and doing the things which the Lord commands without knowing beforehand how He will "bring forth his righteous purposes" (1 Nephi 4:13).

Although we now associate any search for God's "tender mercies" with Nephi, his discernment of and thankfulness for these blessings was learned at Lehi's feet. Long before Nephi reached the promised land and set down his account in the small plates, Lehi taught his son to seek for evidences and to acknowledge the receipt of divine favor. At the beginning of his vision of the tree of life, Lehi finds himself traveling "in a dark and dreary waste . . . for the space of many hours." Seeking relief, Lehi begins "to pray unto the Lord that he would have mercy on me, according to the multitude of his tender mercies," and his petition for relief is immediately answered as he beholds the tree of life and tastes of its fruit (1 Nephi 8:7–8). In sharing this account with his sons, Lehi modeled for them an appropriately meek and thankful response to adversity. His experience in this vision—following a divine messenger clothed in white on what seemed like an interminable and pointless journey—parallels the experience of his sons, who left their comfortable lives in Jerusalem to travel with Lehi in the wilderness. Laman and Lemuel come to regret following their father and complain about his leadership, but when, in the vision, Lehi struggles on his own sojourn, he responds with gratitude. Crucially, his petition to the Lord for succor includes an acknowledgment of "the multitude of his tender mercies." In other words, Lehi's request for relief includes an expression of thanks for blessings already received or witnessed; he asks for aid in faith, confident that he will receive, because he has previously observed that God directs the affairs of men for their temporal and eternal welfare. Gratitude strengthened Lehi's faith and enabled him to secure for himself and his family the blessings that God was willing to grant but which had been made conditional on his asking for them. Lehi's example of gratitude also taught Nephi to recognize "the tender mercies of the Lord" and endure his own trials with faith and thanksgiving.

Lehi's prayer of thanks provides a pattern for us, like Nephi, as we seek to cultivate the spiritual gift of gratitude in our lives. Giving thanks in prayer schools our hearts and minds, allowing the Holy Ghost to instruct us about the nature and number of God's tender mercies in our lives. Consider an experience related by Elder Bednar, describing an incident that occurred during his service as the president of Brigham Young University-Idaho, when he was hosting a visiting Apostle:

> Earlier in the day Sister Bednar and I had been informed about the unexpected death of a dear friend, and our immediate desire was to pray for the surviving spouse and children. As I invited my wife to offer the prayer, the member of the Twelve, unaware of the tragedy, graciously suggested that in the prayer Sister Bednar express only appreciation for blessings received and ask for nothing. His counsel was similar to Alma's instruction to the members of the ancient Church "to pray without ceasing, and to give thanks in all things."

Sister Bednar responded in faith to this inspired invitation, giving thanks for the life of their friend, for the atoning sacrifice of Jesus Christ, and for gospel ordinances that bind families together. As a result, the Bednars were taught by the Holy Ghost and received significant new "insights concerning the things about which we should pray and appropriately ask in faith." Concluding his story with counsel, Elder Bednar recommended "that periodically you and I offer a prayer in which we only give thanks and express gratitude. Ask for nothing; simply let our souls rejoice and strive to communicate appreciation with all the energy of our hearts."[3] Those who seek to cultivate the spiritual gift of gratitude will find that such prayers stimulate greater feelings of thanksgiving and help establish a habit of regularly acknowledging the Lord's merciful hand in our lives.

As Lehi recognizes the Lord's tender mercies in his life, his gratitude is made manifest in three distinct stages. First he *feels* grateful; then he *expresses* his thanks; and finally he *demonstrates* his gratitude. Each of these steps represents a deepening or intensification of Lehi's thanksgiving. As we imitate his example by feeling, expressing, and demonstrating gratitude, our hearts will turn to God in thanksgiving with more regularity and a greater intensity.

The progressive stages of Lehi's gratitude are most clearly evident in his response to the safe return of his sons from Jerusalem, where they had been sent on a dangerous mission to obtain the plates of brass from Laban. Nephi writes that when he and his brothers arrived, having completed their errand successfully,

---

3 David A. Bednar, "Pray Always," *Ensign* or *Liahona*, Nov. 2008.

Lehi "was filled with joy, and also my mother, Sariah, was exceedingly glad" (1 Nephi 5:1). Lehi and Sariah feel thankful for the safety of their family and for the acquisition of the brass plates, and then they express that thanks, elevating their vision to acknowledge and honor the source of these blessings. Sariah declares, "I also know of a surety that the Lord hath protected my sons, and delivered them out of the hands of Laban, and given them power whereby they could accomplish the thing which the Lord hath commanded them," and then "they did rejoice exceedingly, and did offer sacrifice and burnt offerings unto the Lord; and they gave thanks unto the God of Israel" (1 Nephi 5:8–9). Lehi and Sariah express their gratitude both verbally and materially, placing a physical symbol of their thanks on the altar as a complement to their words of praise and rejoicing. After expressing thanks in word and deed, Lehi demonstrates his gratitude for the plates of brass by devoting significant time and attention to their study. Nephi writes that when "they had given thanks unto the God of Israel, my father, Lehi, took the records which were engraven upon the plates of brass, and he did search them from the beginning" (1 Nephi 5:10). Even more than his verbal expression of faith, the quantity of time that Lehi allocates to scripture study and the energy with which he shares and applies their teachings show a sincere and lasting gratitude for this received blessing. His example of feeling, expressing, and then demonstrating gratitude provides a pattern for those who seek to develop and perfect this spiritual gift.

Although a sense of gratitude often seems involuntary or innate, and our natural inclination might be to focus on expressing or demonstrating gratitude, the scriptures clearly warn that we must first school our feelings. Giving insincere thanks when we do not feel grateful is a practice fraught with danger. Consider, for example, the case of Cain. His sacrifice, like Abel's, was ostensibly an expression of thanks, but because "Cain loved Satan more than God," his offering was a lie—a profession of feelings he did not actually possess (Moses 5:18). For this reason, God rejected his offering, and He will likewise reject our insincere expressions of gratitude. Mormon admonishes that our prayers and other expressions of gratitude must be offered earnestly,

> for if he offereth a gift, or prayeth unto God, except he shall do it with real intent it profiteth him nothing. For behold, it is not counted unto him for righteousness. For behold, if a man being evil giveth a gift, he doeth it grudgingly; wherefore it is counted unto him the same as if he had retained the gift; wherefore he is counted evil before God. And likewise also it

> is counted evil unto a man, if he shall pray and not with real intent of heart; yea, and it profiteth him nothing, for God receiveth none such. (Moroni 7:6–9)

Before we can appropriately express and demonstrate our gratitude for blessings received, we must first educate our emotions. Only when we sincerely appreciate the gifts of God will we be able to voice our thanks properly.

Of course we should, and must, learn to give thanks in times of hardship, when we may feel that we have nothing in our lives for which to be grateful, just as we have been instructed to pray when we may not feel like praying: "Pray even when you have no desire to pray. . . . That is when you most need to pray."[4] This counsel from Elder Richard G. Scott should inspire us to give thanks even when we may not feel like giving thanks; that is when we most need to express gratitude. But instead of giving thanks insincerely, like Cain, for circumstances or events that do not currently inspire us with feelings of appreciation, we should begin by thanking God for that for which we *are* genuinely grateful. Our most modest efforts in this regard will be answered with the blessing of an expanded perspective, allowing us to feel grateful for more and more in our lives, until we can rejoice even in our afflictions and infirmities.

Feelings of gratitude, like feelings of hope and love and joy, can be cultivated. When, for example, Lehi welcomed home his sons, he might have focused on the negative aspects of their story and nurtured feelings of worry, disappointment, and resentment. He might have worried that Laban's murder would draw search parties after them, expressed disappointment in his older sons for their abuse of Nephi and Sam, or felt resentful that Zoram had been thrust into their family circle without his foreknowledge and consent. Indeed, he almost certainly experienced one or more of these negative feelings when his sons returned with the plates. Our emotions in mortality are rarely unalloyed, pure expressions of joy or sorrow or gratitude. There are almost always multiple feelings competing for our attention and nurture, but we can shape our experience of an individual event—and, iteratively, mortality itself—by choosing which emotions deserve our time and energy.[5] If, when confronted with challenges and hardship, we will sincerely search out reasons to give thanks, no matter how small, our capacity to recognize God's blessings and to feel grateful will increase. To paraphrase Alma, we need only exercise a particle of gratitude, and even if we can do no more than

---

4 Richard G. Scott, "Using the Supernal Gift of Prayer," *Ensign* or *Liahona*, May 2007.
5 For a review of the science investigating how our attention to specific emotions, events, and ideas shapes our experience of reality, see Winifred Gallagher, *Rapt: Attention and the Focused Life* (New York: Penguin Press, 2009).

desire to give thanks, that desire will work in our hearts until gratitude fills our souls (see Alma 32:27). Lehi found reasons to give thanks and, when confronted with challenging circumstances, chose to nurture feelings of gratitude.

Choosing gratitude over fear or frustration is, at least in part, a matter of choosing an anchor or reference point against which to measure our own expectations and experiences. Comparing an area of weakness in our lives to the strengths of others might be depressing, and a popular proverb declares, "Comparison is the thief of joy." But if, instead, we compare our circumstances with the challenges and misfortunes experienced by others, comparison might offer us reason to rejoice. For example, my very young children were wont to complain and rebel whenever they were served split pea soup and objected (truthfully) that their friends were never served that dish, much less forced to finish an entire bowlful. However, after a year or more of listening to their complaints, I showed my children news reports describing the malnutrition of children who regularly ate small cakes or cookies made of dirt because they could not afford more nourishing fare. As we participated in a fundraiser for their relief, and as my children learned to pray for those without access to food around the world, their perspective on the evils of pea soup changed dramatically. Choosing a new anchor point against which to measure their experience of pea soup—dirt cookies, rather than the culinary experiences of their friends—changed their feelings and helped stimulate a greater sense of gratitude.

Too often, instead of comparing our circumstances to the experience of those who are less fortunate—and there is always someone less fortunate, who is in need of our service, love, and prayers—we adopt the attitude of Nephi, son of Helaman, who idealized the experiences of the ancestor for whom he was named. Helaman's son lamented,

> Oh, that I could have had my days in the days when my father Nephi first came out of the land of Jerusalem, that I could have joyed with him in the promised land; then were his people easy to be entreated, firm to keep the commandments of God, and slow to be led to do iniquity; and they were quick to hearken unto the words of the Lord—yea, if my days could have been in those days, then would my soul have had joy in the righteousness of my brethren. But behold, I am consigned that these are my days, and that my soul shall be filled with sorrow because of this the wickedness of my brethren. (Helaman 7:7–9)

Nephi, son of Helaman, forgets that he is *still* living in the promised land and might *still* rejoice in that piece of good fortune. His namesake was a refugee whose brothers tried to murder him on multiple occasions, but Nephi, son of Helaman, imagines that Lehi and his sons enjoyed an idyllic, peaceful life free of conflict and defined by righteousness, not "the wickedness of my brethren." In other words, he chooses an anchor point that makes his own experience seem miserable by comparison. However, if Nephi, son of Helaman, had remembered the abuse of Laman and Lemuel or if he had compared his days with those of Abinadi, who endured even greater hardships and faced martyrdom alone, he might have found reason to give thanks for the faithfulness and companionship of his own brother. Comparison need not be the thief of joy; it can, instead, stimulate rejoicing when accompanied by meekness. Gratitude grows when we acknowledge that we are "not yet as Job" and, comparing our circumstances with those of less fortunate individuals, count our many blessings (D&C 121:10).

Once we have successfully cultivated feelings of gratitude, we should sincerely express our thanks both verbally and, when appropriate, materially. Expressions of thanks need not be elaborate. A sincerely spoken word often conveys exactly the same heart-felt sentiment communicated by gifts, cards, and other physical signs of gratitude. Voicing thanks regularly and in simple terms will convey gratitude more effectively than any single, grand gesture, and when material expressions of gratitude are appropriate or required, they can be given without audience or ceremony. During Lehi's dispensation, prayers of thanksgiving were sometimes accompanied by burnt offerings. These sacrifices reflected the understanding that all our material possessions are held in receivership; offerings acknowledged that the "earth is the Lord's, and the fulness thereof," and expressed gratitude for the use of these goods (Psalms 24:1). Although we no longer participate in the burning of offerings, we continue to give material expressions of our gratitude in other forms. To pay tithing, for example, is to recognize that our increase is the gift of God and not a product of our own strength or genius. When we pray, we may express our gratitude verbally for divine assistance received in securing employment or for the food on our tables, but paying tithing is a material expression of thanks for these same blessings, acknowledging that the ability to earn a living and acquire sustenance comes as a gift from God. Once we have nurtured feelings of gratitude in our hearts, conveying our thanks to God and to others who have blessed our lives—to family, friends, neighbors, and casual acquaintances—is a natural next step. As we increase the frequency and fervency with which we communicate gratitude, the feelings nurtured in our hearts begin to shape how others perceive their environment and themselves in a virtuous cycle that will stimulate both them and us to undertake additional good works.

Good works should also be an outgrowth of gratitude in our own lives; unless our feelings and expressions of thanksgiving prompt us to action, they are in vain. To return to my original example, if Lehi had never read the brass plates, his prayers giving thanks for their acquisition would have been empty words, offered in vain. Only a change in behavior—searching the scriptures "from the beginning"—could adequately demonstrate his deep and abiding gratitude (1 Nephi 5:10). Too often, we think of communicating thanks as a culminating experience, after which our obligation to the giver is ended. But as Elder Bednar taught with respect to prayer, true gratitude entails a "necessity to not only express but to do . . . the requirement to communicate and to act."[6] Like faith, gratitude is a principle of action, and sincere expressions of thanks should be confirmed by deeds demonstrating the depth and duration of our feelings.

I give here three examples of language frequently overheard in prayers offered by Latter-day Saints together with a reflection, for each, on what it might mean to act in demonstration of the gratitude we so commonly profess:

- **We thank you for this food.** Some version of this phrase is habitually uttered by most members before every meal, but in many prosperous households, food is treated more like a disposable commodity than a gift from God. One of the enduring memories of my childhood is of sitting at the dining room table with my grandfather Richard Glass who had endured the hardships and food shortages of the Great Depression. He so thoroughly cleaned his plate at each meal, collecting each crumb with his fork and mopping up gravy or sauces with a piece of bread, that when his plate was placed in the sink, it always looked as if it had already been washed. On one occasion, when I rose to remove my own plate from the table without first finishing all the food that I had been served, he barked at me, ordering me to sit down and finish eating. He probably should have shown greater patience and kindness to a small child in need of correction, but I will never forget his reverence for food; my grandfather's behavior demonstrated his gratitude for each meal far more eloquently than any prayer. Minimizing food waste, paying a generous fast offering so that others might eat, and growing our own fruits or vegetables in a garden are only a few of the many actions that might demonstrate the gratitude we so frequently profess for our food.

---

6 David A. Bednar, "Ask in Faith," *Ensign* or *Liahona*, May 2008.

- **We thank you for the missionaries.** Members of the Church regularly give thanks for the service of full-time missionaries around the world. These expressions of appreciation reflect an understanding of the key role that these consecrated servants play in building up the kingdom of God on the earth and establishing Zion. However, both the missionaries for whom we give thanks and the God to whom we pray would rejoice if, in addition to expressing gratitude, we also demonstrated an attitude of thanksgiving by participating alongside full-time missionaries in the work of finding, teaching, and fellowshipping. Such an approach might begin with prayers for the courage to open our mouths and testify of truth, or it might entail prayerfully committing, in partnership with the Lord, to find someone willing to hear the missionary message by a specific date. These and other, similar actions would demonstrate our gratitude for both the gospel and the gift of missionary service.
- **We thank you for the temple.** Individuals fortunate enough to live in proximity to a temple often give thanks for the blessing of access to its saving and exalting ordinances or for the divine influence which permeates the homes and communities in its shadow. These feelings and expressions of gratitude should lead us to action. Members might demonstrate their appreciation for the temple by preparing the names of deceased family members for ordinances; participating in worldwide efforts to preserve genealogical records so that others might seek out their ancestors; worshipping frequently in the temple; or serving as temple ordinance workers. Such steps show our appreciation for the blessings of temple worship more eloquently than our most fervent prayers.

Our Father in Heaven is surely pleased when we cultivate feelings of gratitude and express our thanks both to Him and to others for blessings received. But we must never be content with mere professions of thanksgiving, lest we incur the condemnation of Isaiah, who "prophesied of you hypocrites, as it is written, This people honoureth me with their lips, but their heart is far from me" (Mark 7:6).

I was first warned against empty, hypocritical expressions of gratitude by a wise Primary teacher named Don Burford, who was called to teach a class full of energetic boys. Each year, for seven years, Brother Burford was called as my teacher and, eventually, as my Scout leader; he lavished time and attention on our class, hosting parties, organizing camping trips, and incentivizing spiritual learning with treats or small gifts. In a lesson that has lingered with me for decades,

Brother Burford used the acronym FED to teach us that gratitude must be felt, expressed, and demonstrated. Like Lehi, Brother Burford exemplified the spiritual gift of gratitude. Despite significant hardships, he lived in a constant spirit of thanksgiving; although he struggled with obesity, related health problems, and romantic disappointments that left him lonely for many years, he exuded a sense of cheery optimism and gratitude. Indeed, I only realized how difficult his life must have been decades later, as an adult, when he spoke to me with some frankness of the disappointments and difficulties he had suffered in life. Even that communication was offered in a spirit of gratitude, as Brother Burford thanked me and my friends for providing him the opportunity to serve us. His life provided a pattern for the Primary lesson he taught on feeling, expressing, and demonstrating our appreciation for the tender mercies of a loving Father in Heaven.

Of course, even those who have carefully cultivated the spiritual gift of gratitude will occasionally fail to exude a spirit of thanksgiving. Lehi, for example, struggled to maintain his faith in God's goodness when he received the news that Nephi's steel bow had broken. As a result of that misfortune, the entire company "did suffer much for the want of food," and Lehi "was truly chastened because of his murmuring against the Lord, insomuch that he was brought down into the depths of sorrow" (1 Nephi 16:19, 25). While Lehi possessed the spiritual gift of gratitude, he was not perfect in its use; only Jesus the Anointed, Giver of Gifts, endured the challenges of mortality in a constant state of thanksgiving.

Jesus urges us on to perfection, but He knows that we will stumble. We may temporarily disqualify ourselves from receiving His gifts, but repentance restored Lehi—and will restore us—to confidence in the Giver. After repenting, Lehi helped his son receive revelation concerning where he should hunt, and when Nephi returned to their tents with food, Lehi led his people to "humble themselves before the Lord, and did give thanks unto him" (1 Nephi 16:32). The same spirit of thanksgiving that had animated Lehi's first weeks in the wilderness returned with repentance. Like other gifts, the spiritual gift of gratitude is not conditional on our perfection in its use but upon our willingness to repent and be perfected through the Atonement of Jesus Christ—and that is a truth for which we all ought to give thanks.

CHAPTER 6
ABISH AND THE GIFT OF GATHERING

ALTHOUGH WE OFTEN CELEBRATE AMMON'S work as a missionary among the Lamanites, some of the credit for his success in teaching and baptizing the people of King Lamoni should be shared with Abish—a remarkable Lamanite woman whose efforts magnified the impact of Ammon's message. When Ammon arrived in Lamoni's household, he offered to labor as a servant. Embedded in the king's household, Ammon tended the royal flocks, fed Lamoni's horses, and performed other menial tasks. Only after the Lord sustained him in a remarkable skirmish, during which he singlehandedly defended the king's flocks from a band of raiders, did Ammon preach the gospel. Impressed by his prowess in battle, Lamoni asked Ammon to identify the source of his power and, moved by his teaching, cried "unto the Lord, saying: O Lord, have mercy; according to thy abundant mercy which thou hast had upon the people of Nephi, have upon me, and my people" (Alma 18:41). Immediately after offering this heartfelt prayer, Lamoni sank into a swoon that lasted for days; indeed, many assumed that he was dead. But on the day appointed for his burial, the king rose to testify of Jesus Christ and His redemptive power. Listening to Lamoni's message, the queen, Ammon, and all the servants in the royal household were so overcome with the Spirit that they, too, fell to the floor, insensible and wrapped up in heavenly visions. Only Abish remained conscious and ambulatory—she was the one witness who knew why the royal family and their servants, including Ammon, were lying on the floor, insensible.

Because her father had told her of a vision he experienced, Abish had "been converted unto the Lord for many years" and recognized that the other members of the royal household had been felled by "the power of God." Correctly "supposing that this opportunity, by making known unto the people what had happened among them, that by beholding this scene it would cause them to believe in the power of God, therefore she ran forth from house to house, making it known unto the people" (Alma 19:16–17). Thus, when Ammon and Lamoni and his wife, the queen, arose from their visions of angels, they found themselves surrounded by a multitude which Abish "had caused . . . to be gathered together" (Alma 19:28). Because this crowd arrived in time to see the king, the queen, and their servants stand up, after "they all lay there as though they were dead," many listened to the gospel message and were converted (Alma 19:18). Ammon's success among the people of Lamoni was amplified by the labors of Abish; without her efforts to assemble a crowd, none would have witnessed this dramatic tableau that prepared the multitude to learn about Jesus Christ. The miracle of mass conversion was brought about by a collaborative exercise of spiritual gifts: the gift of visions, received by Abish's father; Ammon's gift for wielding the sword of justice in defense of truth and virtue; the queen's gift of "exceeding faith"; and the gift of gathering, exercised by Abish herself (Alma 19:10). No single member of the body of Christ could have accomplished this mighty work; it required a confluence of complementary gifts. The Lamanite converts who joined the body of Christ would come to be known as "the people of Ammon" or "Ammonites," but those titles tend to minimize or erase the significant contributions of those who labored alongside Ammon to effect their spiritual rebirth (Alma 27:26; 57:6). The role played in this miracle by Abish, whom God prepared for her part in these events long before Ammon even considered serving a mission among the Lamanites and who kept the faith in silent solitude for years, warrants both admiration and examination. Because all followers of Christ are charged with sharing His gospel, her spiritual gift of gathering is an aptitude that each of us should seek to acquire.

To liken this story of mass conversion to our own circumstances, we could say that Ammon plays the role of a full-time missionary while Abish is, in modern parlance, the only member living in a new area that Ammon has been called to open for the work of salvation. The miraculous conversion of so many was a direct result of member and missionary working together; neither Ammon nor Abish, missionary nor member, could have accomplished this work on their own. Full-time missionaries frequently study this account to better understand the reasons for Ammon's success, hoping to replicate the miraculous outcomes he enjoyed among Lamoni's people. However, the earnest efforts of missionaries seeking to imitate Ammon will never bear fruit unless the members among whom they live and serve are similarly willing to study the example of Abish. In search of investigators eager to be taught the gospel of Jesus Christ, full-time missionaries have often traveled from house to house, hoping to find receptive hearts. However, in this story, it is not Ammon the missionary but Abish the member who "ran forth from house to house," gathering a crowd. This pattern, in which members gather and missionaries teach, is consonant with principles taught by Elder David A. Bednar, who observed that

> a common element in many of our prayers is a request that the missionaries will be led to individuals and families who are prepared to receive the message of the Restoration. But ultimately it is my responsibility and your responsibility to find people for the missionaries to teach. Missionaries are full-time teachers; you and I are full-time finders. And you and I as lifelong missionaries should not be praying for the full-time missionaries to do our work![1]

To study the example of Abish and seek for the spiritual gift of gathering is to take a first step in fulfilling our responsibility to find individuals willing to be taught by the full-time missionaries.

Although we might naturally focus on her actions in running from house to house, Abish succeeded because of who she was as much as what she did; the gift of gathering is manifest in our character as well as our behavior. Consider the nature of her task: Abish moved quickly, running from house to house, and at each domicile, she had to convince the inhabitants to drop everything and immediately relocate to Lamoni's palace. The scriptures clearly indicate that those arriving at the palace did not understand what had happened to the king and his household or why they were congregating. When the multitude "began to assemble themselves together unto the house of the king. . . . To their astonishment, they beheld the king, and the queen, and their servants prostrate upon the earth" (Alma 19:18). Both "their astonishment" and the speculation that follows indicate their ignorance; as members of the crowd observe the fallen members of the royal household, they converse, "some saying that it was a great evil that had come upon them, or upon the king and his house, because he had suffered that the Nephite should remain in the land," while others opined that "the king hath brought this evil upon his house, because he slew his servants who had had their flocks scattered at the waters of Sebus," and a third group blamed Ammon himself (Alma 19:19–21). Although Abish persuaded many to come to the palace, she could not explain to each, or to any, what had happened—the explanation would have taken so long that she could never have reached a sufficient number of households to draw a crowd.

---

1 David A. Bednar, "Ask in Faith," *Ensign* or *Liahona*, May 2008.

All she could do, as she ran from house to house, was tell the inhabitants that something incredible had happened at the palace and invite them to assemble there immediately.

That so many heeded her invitation and came at once is a testament to her character more than the efficacy of her methods. As full-time missionaries will attest, knocking on the doors of strangers to declare that you have an urgent and life-changing message is not generally an effective means of sharing the gospel—or any other news. Imagine someone arriving at your home or place of employment, out of breath, to tell you that you need to stop what you are doing and walk a mile or more to the seat of local government, where you will see something unbelievable but incredibly important. Then, before you can ask any questions, you see the messenger run off to deliver the same slightly incoherent message at another home or business. Would you drop everything and do what the messenger said? The answer almost certainly depends on who is delivering the message. If the messenger is a complete stranger, you would likely laugh and return to the task from which he or she had distracted you; only someone you already know and trust could deliver such a message and realistically expect you to respond. The people listened to Abish precisely because she was *not* a stranger. She arrived at their homes as a friend, someone whose past behavior identified her as a trustworthy and reliable source of information.

In its broad strokes—a messenger pressed for time successfully gathers a crowd to participate in life-changing events—the story of Abish parallels another episode in American history: the midnight ride of Paul Revere. Learning that British soldiers would march to confiscate a stockpile of colonial munitions, Revere rode at night from Boston, Massachusetts, through Charlestown, Medford, North Cambridge, and Menotomy to the towns of Concord and Lexington, waking the colonists as he passed through each town with a plea to gather and oppose this act of aggression. Like Abish, Revere had no time for extended explanations; he needed the people of Massachusetts to respond immediately, without questioning the urgency of his message or the reliability of his information, and like Abish, Revere succeeded because of his character, because of who he *was* as much as what he *did* on that night. He had friends or business associates in each of these towns, people willing to trust and act on his message without prolonged discussion or explanations. The size of their social circle and the strength of their relationships with each member of that circle enabled both Abish and Revere to gather crowds primed for action. In *The Tipping Point*, a book that asks how ideas spread from one person to another, Malcolm Gladwell describes Revere and similar individuals as "Connectors, people with a special gift for bringing the world together" that have "a truly extraordinary knack of making friends and acquaintances."[2] Abish and Revere were each successful in assembling a crowd not, primarily, because of their efforts in the moment, as they moved from house to house, but because of prior years spent interacting and developing relationships of trust with broad swaths of their communities.

The work of gathering, in other words, occurs longitudinally, over the course of time, as individuals like Abish and Revere cultivate ties to diverse swaths of their community; the actual assemblage of a crowd on a given day is almost perfunctory—a predictable effect of such individuals speaking to the dozens or even hundreds of people in their social circle. Dale Carnegie describes another connector who, over the course of years, came to know more than fifty thousand people on a first-name basis. Working first as a salesman and then as a town clerk, James Farley

> built up a system for remembering names. In the beginning, it was a very simple one. Whenever he met a new acquaintance, he found out his or her complete name and some facts about his or her family, business and political opinions. He fixed all these facts well in mind as part of the picture, and the next time he met that person, even if it was a year later, he was able to shake hands, inquire after the family, and ask about the hollyhocks in the backyard. No wonder he developed a following![3]

Farley would use his gift for gathering individuals to a cause in American politics, serving as the campaign manager for Franklin Delano Roosevelt's successful presidential bids in 1932 and 1936. His example serves as both a warning and a model for those who wish to follow in Abish's footsteps and learn to gather more effectively over the course of years.

For disciples of Jesus Christ, the purpose of gathering can never be the acquisition of a personal following. Nephi admonishes readers of the Book of Mormon that those who seek personal fame and fortune by presenting themselves as standards of goodness, success, or wisdom are guilty of priestcraft, "for, behold, priestcrafts are that men preach and set themselves up for a light unto the world, that they may get gain and praise of the world; but they seek not the

---

2 Malcolm Gladwell, *The Tipping Point: How Little Things Can Make a Big Difference* (New York: Little, Brown and Co., 2000), 38, 41.
3 Dale Carnegie, *How to Win Friends and Influence People*, rev. ed. (New York: Pocket Books, 1981), 72.

welfare of Zion. Behold, the Lord hath forbidden this thing," and if ever an observer has cause to say of us, as Carnegie says of Farley, that we have developed a following, it is a cautionary sign that we may have turned His gifts to an improper use. In order to guard against this cult of the self, Nephi explains, "the Lord God hath given a commandment that all men should have charity, which charity is love. And except they should have charity they were nothing. Wherefore, if they should have charity they would not suffer the laborer in Zion to perish. But the laborer in Zion shall labor for Zion; for if they labor for money they shall perish" (2 Nephi 26:29–31). Gathering must be motivated by the love of Christ, which always redirects our focus to the last, the lost, and the least, those most in need of our time, attention, and means. Our labor as gatherers must always be for the building up of Zion, the kingdom of God on the earth.

As we pursue that holy purpose and seek for the gift of gathering, Farley offers an example worthy of our imitation. His methods provide a pattern for the practical application of scriptural principles given by Moroni for the gathering of Zion. Speaking of new converts, Moroni recalls that

> after they had been received unto baptism, and were wrought upon and cleansed by the power of the Holy Ghost, they were numbered among the people of the church of Christ; and their names were taken, that they might be remembered and nourished by the good word of God, to keep them in the right way, to keep them continually watchful unto prayer, relying alone upon the merits of Christ, who was the author and the finisher of their faith. And the church did meet together oft, to fast and to pray, and to speak one with another concerning the welfare of their souls. (Moroni 6:4–5)

Farley numbered his friends and acquaintances by the thousands, and he knew the names and circumstances of each. When he met one in the street or sat down to write a handwritten note, as he often did, he could speak concerning the welfare of their golf game, their hollyhocks, or their family members. We often profess, in the Church, to care about the welfare of souls, but those we are charged to number and name too frequently remain anonymous; we know less about the lives of those with whom we worship than Farley knew about a stranger he met in passing, while traveling through a city on business. You and I may not have the capacity to remember the biographical details of fifty thousand acquaintances, but we *are* capable of knowing and naming our neighbors and every member of the congregations we attend weekly.

If each member of the ward you attend walked past you, in a line, how many could you name? To what percentage of those you name could you ask a meaningful question about their work, hobbies, or family members? Until and unless we care for others in this small way, our efforts to gather will always be in vain. When, as a newly ordained elder, I arrived at Brigham Young University, I was almost immediately set apart as the president of an elders quorum. I busied myself with the work of organizing home teaching routes, planning Sunday lessons, and attending ward council meetings. As I accomplished those duties efficiently, I felt a glow of satisfaction at having done all I was supposed to do. But that feeling of contentment disappeared when, on the final Sunday of the semester, I stood at the door of our classroom to welcome each member of the quorum to our meeting. As I welcomed each elder, I realized, to my embarrassment, that there were at least two men I could not greet by name; although I had served as their elders quorum president for months, I could not readily identify all of the sheep for whom Heavenly Father had given me responsibility. That failure to gather in God's way lingered with me for many months. It was the cause of considerable anguish and much repentance as I felt the chastisement of the Holy Ghost. I came to know in a deeply personal way that the Lord regards the call to name and number and nourish His children as one of our most significant duties.

When I returned to BYU after serving a mission that ended prematurely, for health reasons, I was given another lesson in the value of gathering others in the manner described by Moroni. Prior to my mission, I had declared a major in English and enrolled in a course on literary theory. On the first day of class, my instructor—a diminutive but craggy old man named Steve Walker—asked each of the twenty-five students seated before him to stand, announce his or her name, and share one interesting biographical detail. When all the students had introduced themselves, he repeated back to us, in rapid succession, our names and the personal information we had shared with him. Astounded, we broke into spontaneous applause. Steve (who insisted that we call him by his first name) had displaced the disorienting, anonymous experience of arriving at a large university with an intimate encounter that communicated his interest in each of us as individuals. Still, he remembered our names so effortlessly that I could not help but wonder if his performance was more parlor trick than an expression of enduring interest in our lives. Two years after that class had ended, when I returned to BYU with a case of clinical depression, I learned the answer. As I hobbled on crutches along the hallway of a building that had not existed when I left on my mission, Steve saw me from more than a hundred feet away and called out my name. Rushing to my side, he peppered me with questions about my injury and invited me into his office for a chat that turned into a tearful, hour-long discussion of my doubts and insecurities. That interaction, in which I learned that Steve truly cared about me, was life changing. In calling me by name and speaking, at length, about my physical, emotional, and spiritual welfare, he gathered me to a path of discipleship that continues to define important aspects of my personal and professional life. If, like Paul Revere and Abish, Steve had asked me (or, I suspect, any of the thousands of students he taught) to drop everything and come running, I would have responded immediately—not because of the words he spoke in that moment but because I had felt the force of his love over the course of several semesters.

The ability of individuals like Steve Walker and James Farley to memorize names and faces in a matter of minutes is truly remarkable. However, such feats of memorization are *expressions* of the spiritual gift of gathering and not the gift itself. Others express their love for individuals and gather them cumulatively, one by one, through different means. Gladwell tells the story of a man named Roger Horchow, whose memory was, perhaps, no better than mine or yours. But whenever Horchow encountered someone with whom he felt a connection, he recorded that individual's address and a few salient facts: "If I met you and like you and you happen to mention your birthday, I write it in and you'll get a birthday card from Roger Horchow."[4] Mailing more than a thousand birthday cards each year helped Horchow maintain a wide web of friendships, but it required little in the way of memory—only a calendar and a willingness to write small notes of encouragement and affection every day.

Like Horchow, my mother, Priscilla Glass Hutchins, has a penchant for sending off birthday cards and notes almost every day, but she also gathers others around and through her dinner table. During my childhood, a week rarely passed without some new guest joining us for a meal. Sometimes she invited new members of our congregation who had just moved into town to be our guests. On other occasions, she would pull over our station wagon to ask individuals who were walking on the side of the road and looked down on their luck whether they wanted to get in the car and come home with us for a hot meal. One memorable morning, my father, who was serving as the town police chief, discharged a vagrant who had spent the night in jail, only

---

4 Gladwell, *The Tipping Point*, 45.

to find the man sitting at his dinner table that night after his wife had found him on the side of the road and offered him a hot meal! In addition to these visitors, more than seventy foster children sat down at our dinner table over the years; many returned to their homes after only a few nights, but some stayed for a decade or more and became permanent members of the family.

Like Abish, my mother was a gatherer, but when she traveled from house to house, she carried a plate of cookies or a pan of cinnamon rolls. During the years my father presided over the Tampa Florida Mission, Priscilla accompanied him to every round of interviews, baking fresh cinnamon rolls to share with the elders and sisters they served. Although these missionaries were required to give an accounting of their ecclesiastical stewardship to my father, they often expressed themselves more fully and frankly to my mother, outside of those formal interviews, because they recognized her cinnamon rolls as an expression of love. Several of her children now invite their own regular, varied cast of dinner guests to sign a special tablecloth after each meal. These tablecloths are visual symbols of the way in which friends, families, and casual acquaintances have been gathered together in love and through food.

The specific means—memorizing names and faces, sending out birthday cards, baking cinnamon rolls—by which we gather others may vary; the Holy Ghost will guide all who seek for this gift in identifying appropriate methods for helping others to feel known and loved. But the scriptures offer clear, consistent guidance on the question of who is to be gathered: everyone. Those who would gather cannot hope to have heaven's help unless they are willing to name and number and love and invite everyone they encounter. During His mortal ministry, the Savior taught that "the kingdom of heaven is like unto a net, that was cast into the sea, and gathered of every kind: which, when it was full, they drew to shore, and sat down, and gathered the good into vessels, but cast the bad away. So shall it be at the end of the world: the angels shall come forth, and sever the wicked from among the just" (Matthew 13:47–49). There will, eventually, be a sorting or judgment during which the righteous will be gathered into one kingdom and the wicked into another, but that selective gathering is the work of God and His angels, during the last judgment. Until that day, fishers of men must be indiscriminate, gathering "of every kind." Christ is clear on this point: "he inviteth them all to come unto him and partake of his goodness; and he denieth none that come unto him, black and white, bond and free, male and female; and he remembereth the heathen; and all are alike unto God, both Jew and Gentile" (2 Nephi 26:33). Our natural inclination might be to gather those who are like ourselves or to invite individuals who fit the social profile of a stereotypical Latter-day Saint, but God has made it clear that all must be offered the gospel. To ancient Israel, He instructed that "eunuchs" and "the sons of the stranger"—those who might otherwise have been instinctively shunned—must be invited to "join themselves to the Lord. . . . For mine house shall be called an house of prayer for all people. The Lord God which gathereth the outcasts of Israel saith, Yet will I gather others to him, beside those that are gathered unto him" (Isaiah 56:3–8). The gift of gathering can only be exercised by those willing to love, name, and number "all people"—not just those who fit a certain stereotype.

This indiscriminate ethos is modeled in our approach to temple and family history work. We offer the ordinances of salvation and exaltation to all, posthumously, without inquiring into the circumstances of their lives to determine whether we think they would have accepted the message of the Restoration during their time on earth. There are no background checks required of our ancestors. We may ultimately, because of choices made by others, gather just "one of a city, and two of a family," as Jeremiah prophesied, but gospel blessings must be offered to every inhabitant of a city, every member of a family (Jeremiah 3:14). The outreach of Dong Hun Choi in South Korea exemplified a desire to invite or gather all, on both sides of the veil. Choi's son, Elder Yoon Hwan Choi, shared an account of his father's missionary and family history efforts in general conference:

> After work he went with the missionaries to visit our family, friends, and neighbors nearly every day. Seven months after we were baptized, 23 of my family and relatives became members of the Church. That was followed by the miracle of seeing 130 people baptized in the following year through my father's member missionary work.
>
> Family history was also important to him, and he completed eight generations of our ancestors. From that time on, the fruits of our family conversion, started by my 14-year-old brother, have increased in countless ways not only among the living but also among the dead. Building upon the work of my father and others, our family tree now spans to 32 generations, and we are now completing temple work for many branches.[5]

Elder Choi's father gathered—or attempted to gather—everyone. He did not decide beforehand which cousins or ancestors or neighbors or friends would

---

5 Yoon Hwan Choi, "Don't Look Around, Look Up!" *Ensign* or *Liahona*, May 2017.

accept the gospel. Similarly, our work is not to intuit which family members or which neighbors will progress along the covenant path; we simply gather all who are willing to be gathered.

The same spirit of universal outreach that motivated Dong Hun Choi has also characterized the apostolic ministry of President Russell M. Nelson. Speaking shortly after President Nelson was sustained as the seventeenth prophet of this dispensation, Elder Gary E. Stevenson testified that the prophet's "outreach is to all, young and old. He seems to know everyone and is particularly gifted at remembering names. All who know him feel that they are his favorite. And so it is with each of us—because of his genuine love and concern for everyone."[6] When, days later, President Nelson embarked on a tour of the Church that would take him to see Saints on four continents, he declared, "The Lord's message is for everyone. This is a global work. Whenever I'm comfortably situated in my home, I'm in the wrong place. I need to be where the people are."[7] Even more than his numerous voyages to visit Church members around the world or his facility with names, this attitude of loving outreach identifies President Nelson as one whose life exemplifies the gift of gathering. As an Apostle, Elder Nelson invited each of us to join with him in this work, pleading with Church members to "reach out to those you do not know and greet them warmly. Each Sunday extend a hand of fellowship to at least one person you did not know before. Each day of your life, strive to enlarge your own circle of friendship."[8] The average member may not have President Nelson's gift for remembering names, but if we follow his counsel, both our circle of friends and our capacity to gather will surely grow.

Significantly, our success as gatherers is not predicated on outcomes, on the number of our acquaintances who make baptismal covenants, or on the percentage of our ancestors who accept covenants we make on their behalf in the temple. The gift of gathering will not guarantee a string of convert baptisms and the return of wayward friends or children. Consider the disappointment of Jesus Christ as He assessed the results of His own efforts to spiritually gather the descendants of Lehi:

> O ye people of these great cities which have fallen, who are descendants of Jacob, yea, who are of the house of Israel, how oft have I gathered you as a hen gathereth her chickens under her wings, and have nourished you.

---

6 Gary E. Stevenson, "The Heart of a Prophet," *Ensign* or *Liahona*, May 2018.

7 Russell M. Nelson's Facebook page, post from Apr. 13, 2018, https://www.facebook.com/lds.russell.m.nelson/.

8 Russell M. Nelson, "Be Thou an Example of the Believers," *Ensign* or *Liahona*, Nov. 2010.

> And again, how oft would I have gathered you as a hen gathereth her chickens under her wings, yea, O ye people of the house of Israel, who have fallen; yea, O ye people of the house of Israel, ye that dwell at Jerusalem, as ye that have fallen; yea, how oft would I have gathered you as a hen gathereth her chickens, and ye would not.
>
> O ye house of Israel whom I have spared, how oft will I gather you as a hen gathereth her chickens under her wings, if ye will repent and return unto me with full purpose of heart.
> (3 Nephi 10:4–6)

Even our God, who gathers perfectly, is regularly disappointed by the decisions of those He loves, who refuse to be gathered. That is why Elder Clayton M. Christensen, an Area Seventy, emphasized that success in gathering has nothing to do with how others respond to our invitation: "*we succeed as member missionaries when we invite people to learn and accept the truth.*"[9] The number of invitations we have extended in the recent past is the best indication of our progress in seeking for the gift of gathering. We may feel prompted to invite friends to meet with the missionaries or to invite strangers to dine at our table; the invitation will vary, but the spirit of gathering should be a constant in our lives. As we learn to name and number and nourish those with whom we come in contact through inspired invitations, the only certain outcome is that we ourselves will be gathered to the Savior and know Him more intimately. That is enough.

So if our first and best efforts to gather do not meet with success, we must not quit or assume, mistakenly, that we have no gift. Elder Christensen warned "that the ability to share the gospel isn't a 'gift' that has been given to only a few Latter-day Saints and denied to the rest"; all have been called to gather, and all may receive direction and power from heaven as we persist in accomplishing that work.[10] In response to the rejection of Lehi's descendants, Jesus Christ returned with a new invitation and promise: "how oft will I gather you." The work of gathering is both longitudinal and iterative, accomplished over the course of time through consistent, loving outreach, irrespective of rejection. For many, the sole evidence of our sincerity and love will be a willingness to persist in nourishing and inviting despite their serial rejections. We cannot expect sweeping, unequivocal success where the Savior Himself has been rebuffed.

---

9 Clayton M. Christensen, *The Power of Everyday Missionaries: The What and How of Sharing the Gospel* (Salt Lake City, UT: Deseret Book, 2012), 24.

10 Christensen, *The Power of Everyday Missionaries*, 13.

Although a great crowd responded to the invitation of Abish, there were "many among them who would not hear [Ammon's] words; therefore they went their way" (Alma 19:32). We should honor Abish and imitate her example in gathering God's children individually, one by one and house by house; but we must also remember that gathering is a gift exercised in faith, whose ultimate outcome is contingent upon the agency of others.

There are, in scripture and in the records of the Restored Church, numerous examples of individuals other than Abish who likewise exercised the gift of gathering. The Samaritan woman with whom Jesus Christ spoke at the well of Sychar was one such, who gathered "many of the Samaritans of that city [who] believed on him for the saying of the woman" (John 4:39). Others were specifically called to the work of gathering. For example, John the Baptist and Sidney Rigdon, who was "sent forth, even as John, to prepare the way" for the Restoration, accrued significant followings through their preaching before pointing those crowds to the message of someone with greater authority (D&C 35:4). This pattern is consistent with the work done by Abish, who collected a crowd and then allowed those in positions of authority—Ammon, Lamoni, and the queen—to take the lead in teaching. But the ability of Abish to assemble a multitude, every bit as effectively as John or Sidney Rigdon, is a welcome reminder that gathering need not be predicated on our eloquence or on rising to a position of social prominence. Abish was a humble servant. Her only contribution, in a tale filled with kings and queens and miracles, was to extend an invitation to everyone she met. However, that invitation was a catalyst that magnified the efforts of Ammon and led to the conversion of thousands. Those thousands became known as Ammonites, not Abishites, but her contribution was essential to their progress along the covenant path.

In a world increasingly plagued by loneliness, the need for men and women like Abish has never been greater.[11] All of us long to be known, to hear others call us by name and invite us to join and participate and gather. Interacting digitally, with virtual friends who we see only rarely—if ever—cannot satisfy the universal desire for meaningful social and spiritual connections. To wander,

---

11 Vivek Murthy, former Surgeon General of the United States, details the prevalence of loneliness and its devastating health impacts in his essay, "Work and the Loneliness Epidemic," *Harvard Business Review*, https://hbr.org/cover-story/2017/09/work-and-the-loneliness-epidemic. See also the research of BYU professor Julianne Holt-Lunstad, whose research laid the groundwork for Murthy's claims.

"lonely as a cloud," is human; to gather and be gathered, divine.[12] There is no gift more godly than the gathering of those who linger, lonely, at the margins of society. Whatever other gifts we may possess, we should all aspire to imitate Abish—to know and name and nourish our neighbors, so that our invitations are received as expressions of love.

---

12 William Wordsworth, "I Wandered Lonely as a Cloud," in *The Poetical Works of William Wordsworth* (London: Edward Moxon, 1847), 144–45. Notwithstanding his praise for the "bliss of solitude," Wordsworth speaks to the desire for a sense of connection in this poem; his joy comes in dancing "with the daffodils" in "jocund company" and not merely in observing them dance.

CHAPTER 7
TEANCUM AND THE GIFT OF BEING ANXIOUSLY ENGAGED

THE WAR CHAPTERS OF ALMA are filled with stories of clever battlefield tactics, as Captain Moroni and his men make the most of relatively scant resources—often in the face of overwhelming numerical odds. Moroni arms the women and children of a prison camp, sends a spy to deliver drugged wine, and fortifies the cities under his protection "in a manner which never had been known among the children of Lehi" (Alma 49:8). Innovation and a willingness to defy convention enabled Nephite war leaders to defeat an enemy intent on their destruction. The soldiers serving under these innovative leaders are often commended for their obedience in carrying out the commands of their superior officers. Famously, the stripling warriors, who come to the army from the people of Ammon and follow Helaman into battle, "obey and observe to perform every word of command with exactness" (Alma 57:21). The prophetic narrators of these stories describe the obedience of these youth as a key to their preservation, as every one of Helaman's soldiers survives the war, notwithstanding their participation in battles with catastrophic casualty rates. Obedience was an essential element in the success of Moroni's army but so, too, was a willingness to innovate, act in the absence of commands, and on occasion, disobey. In other words, their military success was a product of independent thought and action as well as obedience.

On several occasions, Teancum, another of Moroni's commanders, undertook daring nighttime raids of his own accord or altered the plans established by his commanding officer. His actions on these occasions underscore the importance of counsel given many hundreds of years later, in the Doctrine and Covenants:

> For behold, it is not meet that I should command in all things; for he that is compelled in all things, the same is a slothful and not a wise servant; wherefore he receiveth no reward.
>
> Verily I say, men should be anxiously engaged in a good cause, and do many things of their own free will, and bring to pass much righteousness;

> For the power is in them, wherein they are agents unto themselves. (D&C 58:26–28)

Because Teancum was anxiously engaged in a good cause and repeatedly acted of his own accord, in the absence of commands, a devastating war was concluded several years earlier than it might otherwise have ended. His gift for being anxiously engaged—seeking out opportunities when independent action might significantly impact others for good—saved the lives of thousands on both sides of the war.

Teancum was a worrier. But instead of allowing his anxiety for the welfare of others to paralyze him with fear, he took action, both to guard against negative outcomes and to make preemptive strikes that foreshortened the war. Most famously, he decided on two different occasions to infiltrate the Lamanite camp and assassinate a king responsible for instigating or perpetuating the conflict with his people. On the first occasion, "Teancum and his servant stole forth and went out by night, and went into the camp of Amalickiah," the king of the Lamanites. Then Teancum "put a javelin to his heart," killing Amalickiah so swiftly and silently that the king's servants remained asleep (Alma 51:33–34). This raid was a bold stroke undertaken at great personal danger, of Teancum's own volition. Not only was he not commanded to assassinate Amalickiah—a strategy never before employed in Nephite history—but the single servant who accompanied him on this mission was the only person he informed of his plans before carrying them out. Only after he had successfully killed Amalickiah and escaped back "to his own camp," where "his men were asleep," did he wake them "and told them all the things that he had done. And he caused that his armies should stand in readiness, lest the Lamanites had awakened and should come upon them" (Alma 51:35–36). Teancum's anxiety for the welfare of his people led him to undertake a mission of significant strategic importance without the knowledge of his men or the consent of his commanding officer. Worried, after the completion of this mission, that his actions might bring down an unexpected attack, he roused the camp without regard for the popularity of his decision— and given that there was no evidence the Lamanites knew of Amalickiah's death, much less that they were marching in retaliation, it probably was *not* popular. In the absence of modern communications, Teancum chose to proceed without the knowledge or approval of Moroni, acting as an agent unto himself on a potentially perishable opportunity. As a result, the Lamanites "were affrighted; and they abandoned their design in marching into the land northward" (Alma 52:2). By forcing the Lamanites to forsake their offensive, Teancum's actions saved the lives of those who would otherwise have fought in the land northward.

Unfortunately, Amalickiah's death did not end the conflict, as his brother Ammoron assumed the throne and continued to wage the war initiated by

Amalickiah for six more years. At the end of Ammoron's sixth year at the head of the Lamanite armies, Teancum and his men were reunited with the larger army commanded by Moroni and "did encamp with their armies round about . . . insomuch that the Lamanites were encircled about" (Alma 62:34). The pursuit and flanking of Ammoron's army was an exhausting maneuver, and so

> the Nephites and the Lamanites also were weary because of the greatness of the march; therefore they did not resolve upon any stratagem in the night-time, save it were Teancum; for he was exceedingly angry with Ammoron, insomuch that he considered that Ammoron, and Amalickiah his brother, had been the cause of this great and lasting war between them and the Lamanites, which had been the cause of so much war and bloodshed, yea, and so much famine.
>
> And it came to pass that Teancum in his anger did go forth into the camp of the Lamanites, and did let himself down over the walls of the city. And he went forth with a cord, from place to place, insomuch that he did find the king; and he did cast a javelin at him, which did pierce him near the heart. But behold, the king did awaken his servants before he died, insomuch that they did pursue Teancum, and slew him. (Alma 62:35–36)

Although Moroni likely knew and approved of this second nighttime raid, Teancum clearly conceived of and executed the mission on his own. Again, at great personal cost, he took the initiative and acted in the absence of commands to remove a threat to the well-being of his people. As a result, when Moroni marched against the Lamanites the following day, he "did drive them out of the land; and they did flee, even that they did not return at that time against the Nephites" (Alma 62:38). Teancum's sacrifice and his eagerness to serve the Nephite people led to the war's abbreviation. On this occasion, as on others, Teancum's desire to be anxiously engaged brought to pass much righteousness.

Identifying Teancum as a model for our own anxious engagement offers a new perspective on our participation in hierarchical command structures, such as those deployed in The Church of Jesus Christ of Latter-day Saints. Each member of the Church is embedded in ecclesiastical units led by presiding officers—a Relief Society president, a bishop, a teacher's quorum president—who extend callings or assignments to those whom they lead, just as Moroni gave assignments and a specific sphere of responsibility to Teancum, Helaman, and other subordinate officers. Those callings and assignments help to focus our energies on specific tasks necessary for maintaining and enlarging the kingdom of God on the earth. Ideally, when presiding officers extend callings or assignments, they also offer training in how best to accomplish the ultimate objectives of those callings and assignments; they may read from the Church handbook and the scriptures with those receiving assignments, so that "every man [and woman might] learn his [or her] duty, and to act in the office in which he [or she] is appointed, in all diligence" (D&C 107:99). The value of this training, in the accomplishment of our objectives, is evident in Mormon's account of Teancum and his men. When Amalickiah first encounters Teancum, "he met with a disappointment by being repulsed by Teancum and his men, for they were great warriors; for every man of Teancum did exceed the Lamanites in their strength and in their skill of war" (Alma 51:31). That strength and skill was a product of exemplary training. Teancum's military success, and our own success in building up the kingdom of God, depends on a willingness to extend and accept assignments, then undergo training necessary to fulfill those assignments.

Members of the Church generally understand the need for assignments and training. However, we place such emphasis on callings, assignments, and training that those who receive assignments and callings sometimes mistake the duties in which they have been trained as outward limits for their action, rather than a necessary foundation of works facilitating the accomplishment of service and good deeds that may not have been imagined by those who trained them in their duties. For example, in the days of home teaching, priesthood holders were frequently trained in their responsibilities to "visit the house of each member, and exhort them to pray vocally and in secret and attend to all family duties" (D&C 20:47). In urging home teachers to visit the house of all members at least once a month and encourage them in their duties, Church leaders may have unintentionally communicated that such a visit was the only possible way in which home teachers could fulfill their assignments. Thus, Elder Jeffrey R. Holland recounted the true story of two women cleaning a flooded basement on the last day of the month when the doorbell rang, and one woman jokingly suggested that perhaps the other's home teachers had been inspired to visit and help with the cleaning. Her home teachers *had* rung the doorbell and *might* have rendered significant service to this sister for whom they had covenanted to care. But seeing her attired in work clothes, "they said, 'Oh, Molly, we are sorry. We can see you are busy. We don't want to intrude; we'll come another time.' And they were gone."[1] Blinded by their fixation on a specific task, for which they had been trained, these home teachers neglected a perishable chance to serve and bring to pass much righteousness; rather than thinking of their monthly visit as a necessary minimum standard for generating further, more significant service opportunities, they treated it as a constraint. Thus, when Elder Holland later spoke about the abolition of home teaching, he exhorted members that "we should mature personally . . . rising above any mechanical, function-without-feeling routine" to a more flexible and engaged form of personal ministry.[2] Church members, like the stripling warriors and other soldiers who served under Moroni, are to be commended for their diligence in acting on commands—but we should never allow training or routines to limit our involvement in good causes.

Consider, by contrast, the example of a man I will call Ron, who was assigned to serve as a Primary teacher after many years in a high-profile stake calling. The most basic duty of a Primary teacher is simple: teach a brief lesson each Sunday from a manual provided by the Church. But Ron was not content simply to satisfy this minimum requirement; his lessons often included supplementary activities not found in the manual, as when his class of Primary children constructed their own "Titles of Liberty," in imitation of Captain Moroni, and marched around the church building, declaring their commitment to "our God, our religion, and freedom, and our peace" to all they met in the halls (Alma 46:12). In addition to teaching lessons that captured the imaginations of his charges, Ron organized extracurricular outings for the children in his class. He invited each of the families with a child in his class to spend a day on his boat at the local lake. He planned, chaperoned, and paid for a class trip to Palmyra, driving approximately sixteen hours in a single day so that the students in his class could experience the peace of the Sacred Grove and visit the Hill Cumorah. Can you imagine the long-term impact of these outings? When Ron accepted the assignment to teach a Primary class, he fulfilled the expectation that he offer a lesson each Sunday. But he also magnified his calling in meaningful ways without being asked to do so, and his anxious engagement in the lives of Primary children will bear fruit and "bring to pass much righteousness" in the years to come (D&C 58:27).

Magnifying his calling as a Primary teacher is one expression of Ron's gift for being anxiously engaged, but it is hardly the only way in which that gift has been manifest. Members of his ward frequently benefit from acts of service that have nothing to do with his calling. When the steep driveway leading to

---

1 Jeffrey R. Holland, "Emissaries to the Church," *Ensign* or *Liahona*, Nov. 2016.
2 Jeffrey R. Holland, "Be With and Strengthen Them," *Ensign* or *Liahona*, May 2018.

their chapel iced over in a winter storm, Ron grabbed a shovel and a bag of salt, working alone and without being asked to clear the road. When ward boundaries shifted, creating a congregation in which few families had long-established friendships, he organized a rotating dinner group/game night that brought members of the ward closer together in unity and love. When his bishop announced that the full-time missionaries would be baptizing the wife and oldest child of an inactive priest, he took the initiative to inquire as to whether her husband might be qualified to perform those ordinances instead; as a result, this husband and father joined his wife and son in the water, helping them along the covenant path. Each of these good deeds was undertaken on his own initiative, without an assignment or calling that might have compelled Ron to act.

The same spirit of engagement is evident in his civic life, outside the Church. Considering the rising costs of college tuition, Ron solicited donations from individuals and businesses to establish a scholarship fund at a local high school. He ran for positions in local and state government, not because he sought a career in politics but because he hoped to effect meaningful, positive change in his community. Being anxiously engaged is an attitude or mindset that has shaped every facet of Ron's life, as he proactively seeks to lift and bless and serve those within his constantly expanding sphere of influence.

Many of those who would reap the fruits of Ron's efforts and Teancum's nighttime raids were strangers; Ron could not know all of the students who would receive scholarship monies in the coming years, and Teancum could not know all of the men and women and children whose lives would be spared because he brought the war to a close. To be anxiously engaged in good causes is to volunteer time and resources for the benefit of strangers, without being asked. Even in the absence of an obvious, pressing crisis that threatens thousands and thousands of lives, those with the gift of being anxiously engaged will act like Teancum because they, as Larissa Macfarquhar writes, "always feel themselves responsible for strangers—they always feel that strangers, like compatriots in war, are their own people. They know that there are always those as urgently in need as the victims of battle, and they consider themselves conscripted by duty." When Kimberly Brown-White spontaneously decided to donate a kidney, she "had no contact with the man who had received her kidney—she never even knew his name, although the hospital told her the transplant had been a success and he was doing well."[3] No one asked Brown-White to donate her kidney;

---

3 Larissa Macfarquhar, *Strangers Drowning: Grappling with Impossible Idealism, Drastic Choices, and the Overpowering Urge to Help* (New York: Penguin Press, 2015), 10–11, 194.

she simply recognized a need and filled it, without worrying about whether her contributions to this good cause would benefit someone she already knew. Joseph Smith taught that this voluntary outreach to strangers and a proactive engagement in good causes which benefit those outside our immediate circle of influence are signs of our conversion. "A man filled with the love of God," he wrote, "is not content with blessing his family alone, but ranges through the whole world, anxious to bless the whole human race."[4] God does not require suicide missions into the enemy camp or the donation of kidneys, but He does hope that each of us will stop thinking so much about what is required and ask instead—of our own volition, without an assignment—how we might use our time and talents in good causes, to bless the whole human race and bring to pass much righteousness.

Considering the good deeds of Ron, Brown-White, and Teancum might seem to communicate the message that being anxiously engaged requires commitments of your body, time, or talents beyond that which you feel able to offer. But being anxiously engaged is more about your mindset and willingness to act than the resources at your disposal. Those who actively seek for good causes to which they can contribute, "not by constraint, but willingly," will always be taught by the Spirit how they can contribute in building up the Kingdom of God (1 Peter 5:2).

The example of Julia Sand in this regard is instructive. In 1881, Julia Sand was an unmarried woman of thirty-two who had been an invalid for the past five years, during which time "she had felt 'dead and buried.'"[5] In other words, Sand lacked the health, energy, and other resources to engage in good causes with the sort of action taken by Ron, Brown-White, and Teancum; no one would have blamed her if she had continued to convalesce in isolation. But Sand made the most of her limited means and acted on a small scale, with enormous consequences. As Sand rested in her rooms, she read that James Garfield, president of the United States, had been shot. She realized, along with the rest of the country, that when Garfield died (which he did, a few months later), Vice President Chester Arthur would become the nation's chief executive officer. That Arthur might soon be elevated to the presidency was widely regarded as a disaster-in-waiting; he had been chosen as Garfield's running mate only to appease certain factions of the Republican Party and had never before been elected to public office. Widely regarded as a symbol of corrupt, back-room politics, Arthur was even accused

---

4 *Teachings of Presidents of the Church: Joseph Smith* [2007], 426.
5 Candice Millard, *Destiny of the Republic: A Tale of Madness, Medicine, and the Murder of a President* (New York: Doubleday, 2011), 208.

by some of having orchestrated Garfield's assassination so that he could take his place. Arthur had been a thorn in Garfield's side ever since the election and was almost universally despised. Many across the country called for his resignation, hoping that a more honest and competent substitute might be appointed before Garfield succumbed to his injury. During this maelstrom of political chaos, and although she had never before met Arthur, Sand picked up her pen and wrote to the Vice President from her sickbed.

Rather than ask Arthur to resign, Sand urged him to rise to the occasion and become a different, better man. She wrote,

> Your kindest opponents say: "Arthur will try to do right"—adding gloomily—"He won't succeed, though—making a man President cannot change him," . . . But making a man President can change him! Great emergencies awaken generous traits which have lain dormant half a life. If there is a spark of true nobility in you, now is the occasion to let it shine. Faith in your better nature forces me to write to you—but not to beg you to resign. Do what is more difficult & more brave. Reform![6]

Sand's words, and her faith in his ability to change, galvanized Arthur. He rejected the corrupt political allies who had helped him rise to prominence and became a president widely praised for his probity. Historian Candice Millard writes, "When Arthur left the White House . . . he was almost unrecognizable as the man who had been Garfield's running mate and vice president. 'No man ever entered the Presidency so profoundly and widely distrusted,' the well-known journalist Alexander McClure wrote, 'and no one ever retired . . . more generally respected.'"[7] Arthur's transformation has been attributed to Sand's influence; he kept twenty-three of her letters and eventually paid her a personal visit to thank her for expressing faith in him when everyone else believed him destined for failure. Sand was no Teancum. She lacked the bodily strength necessary to assassinate a wicked king, donate a kidney, or drive a car full of energetic children to Palmyra. But, having identified a good cause, she chose to act rather than acquiesce to the prospect of a weak and incompetent president. Her anxious, unsolicited engagement in national affairs changed the

---

6 Letter from Julia Sand to Chester Arthur, August 27, 1881; as quoted in Millard, *Destiny of the Republic: A Tale of Madness, Medicine, and the Murder of a President*, 208–9.

7 Millard, *Destiny of the Republic*, 251–52.

course of Arthur's life and, indirectly, facilitated the abolishment of a corrupt system of political patronage.

Like Julia Sand, Rigmor Heistø was a woman of relatively modest means and social stature whose willingness to act brought her into contact with persons of influence and effected meaningful change. Reading an op-ed in which Georg Fredrik Rieber-Mohn, then Norway's attorney general, lamented the disintegration of family values in their country, Heistø mailed materials introducing Rieber-Mohn to The Church of Jesus Christ of Latter-day Saints. He responded by requesting a meeting with Heistø, during which she suggested that Rieber-Mohn might enjoy visiting Brigham Young University to learn more about the Church. After his visit to Utah in 1998, Rieber-Mohn declared, "I should take the whole Mormon Church [back to Norway] with me and the family life you have, and we would see a rapid decline in all the negative signs developing of which I have spoken." Heistø's letter persuaded a man who previously knew almost nothing of the Church to learn more and become a friend to her faith. On another occasion, Heistø suggested during end-of-semester course evaluations that when her theology professor, Guttorm Fløistad, next taught his "Philosophy of Religions" course, he should include a brief unit on The Church of Jesus Christ of Latter-day Saints. Heistø then approached the mission president serving in Norway (a BYU faculty member) and asked for his help in facilitating a visit to Provo for Fløistad. This visit to BYU persuaded Fløistad that he had "found the most perfect organization, and it is The Church of Jesus Christ of Latter-day Saints." As a result of Heistø's outreach, Fløistad has incorporated his views on the Church into the lectures he gives throughout Norway several hundred times a year, declaring, "Even if you are not interested in religion, the next time two Mormon missionaries knock on your door, let them in. There is much you can learn from the Mormons."[8] Heistø's unsolicited actions have helped to make the Church a respected and well-known institution in her home country.

Anyone can write a letter or make a phone call; being anxiously engaged is a matter of eagerness and enthusiasm, not means. Even the interpersonal outreach of a letter or phone call is not necessary to be anxiously engaged. Those who voluntarily dedicate time and energy to the work of indexing genealogical records or other forms of family history work often do so in solitude, contributing to good causes in the absence of specific assignments and in the privacy of their own homes. Similarly, temple attendance is never compulsory, never reported

---

8 Erlend D. Peterson, "Anxiously Engaged in a Good Cause" [Brigham Young University devotional, Mar. 17, 1998], speeches.byu.edu.

to ecclesiastical leaders; individuals who attend often do so because they possess a "disposition . . . to do good continually" and not to meet a quota (Mosiah 5:2). Everyone—including introverts, invalids, and the impoverished—can be anxiously engaged in the work of the kingdom.

Because good causes abound and all who are willing can contribute, those who receive the gift of being anxiously engaged should also seek earnestly for the complementary gift of restraint. Here, too, Teancum provides a pattern. After his assassination of Amalickiah, "Teancum had received orders to make an attack upon the city of Mulek," which had fallen into Lamanite hands, "and retake it." Accordingly, "Teancum made preparations to make an attack upon the city of Mulek, and march forth with his army against the Lamanites; but he saw that it was impossible that he could overpower them while they were in their fortifications; therefore he abandoned his designs and returned again to the city Bountiful, to wait for the coming of Moroni, that he might receive strength to his army" (Alma 52:16–17). Although Teancum was willing to undertake dangerous missions of his own accord, with little regard for his personal safety, on this occasion, he withdrew from a good cause he had been commanded to accomplish lest he overextend himself. Teancum's strategic retreat reflects the wisdom of counsel given by King Benjamin to all those who enlist in good causes, "such as feeding the hungry, clothing the naked, visiting the sick and administering to their relief." King Benjamin warns such men and women to exercise restraint and "see that all these things are done in wisdom and order; for it is not requisite that a man should run faster than he has strength" (Mosiah 4:26–27). In the absence of restraint and a willingness to ignore some good causes or delay responding to a few of the many claims on our time and talents, anxious engagement quickly leads to exhaustion and overexertion.

Another military leader in the Book of Mormon was a model of restraint from whom we might learn much. Like Teancum, Gideon was a man who took initiative without waiting to be compelled or commanded in his pursuit of good causes; observing the wickedness of King Noah and the long-term negative consequences of his leadership, Gideon "drew his sword, and swore in his wrath that he would slay the king," just as Teancum would later kill both Amalickiah and Ammoron (Mosiah 19:4). But in the very moment that Gideon pursued King Noah and might have overthrown his wicked rule, the king saw a Lamanite army invading the land and cried, "Gideon, spare me, for the Lamanites are upon us, and they will destroy us; yea, they will destroy my people" (Mosiah 19:7). Even in his wrath—hardly an emotional state conducive to good decision-making—Gideon exercised restraint and allowed King Noah to live so that he might lead the people in an orderly response to the Lamanite invasion. Gideon's commitment to a good cause did not blind him to the fact that following through on his plan to overthrow the government at that particular time would have been a disservice to the very people he was hoping to help. Gideon also exercised restraint in the aftermath of his battle with the invading Lamanite army. Once Noah fled into the wilderness with an army, Gideon became the most powerful remaining Nephite leader, and he used that power proactively to search for Noah: "Gideon sent men into the wilderness secretly, to search for the king and those that were with him" (Mosiah 19:18). There, the "men of Gideon" learned that Noah had been killed by the men he had led into the wilderness, and they brought Noah's army home (Mosiah 19:22). At this point, Gideon clearly could have drawn on the personal loyalty of his men and the prevailing anger against Noah to consolidate power and elevate himself to the throne; instead, he acknowledged that Noah's son, Limhi, was a righteous leader, and Gideon served in a subordinate role as a trusted advisor throughout Limhi's reign. Gideon's penchant for independent action was tempered by a healthy sense of restraint, preserving him and his people from the pains of an overzealous pursuit of good causes.[9]

Even the Savior, who was a model of anxious engagement and constantly worked to promote good causes during His mortal service, exercised restraint and established parameters defining the scope of His ministry. When he was approached by a foreign woman alternately identified as "a Greek, a Syrophenician" (Mark 7:26), or "a woman of Canaan" (Matthew 15:22), Jesus responded to her plea for help by declaring, "I am not sent but unto the lost sheep of the house of Israel" (Matthew 15:24). Although He made an exception to this rule, showing mercy to this woman and healing her daughter, Jesus clearly had a well-defined sense of mission; rather than responding to every plea for help, He identified a specific population and a specific cause, then acted on behalf of that group and cause without allowing Himself to be distracted by every possible opportunity to serve. Those who are blessed with the gift of being anxiously engaged in good causes or who seek to develop that gift must also, necessarily, cultivate a capacity for restraint. Without this complementary gift, zeal and anxious engagement will result in burnout or the neglect of core responsibilities.

---

9 In contrast, Limhi's grandfather Zeniff was a man anxiously engaged in good causes who lacked the gift of restraint. Zeniff describes himself as "over-zealous to inherit the land of our fathers" (Mosiah 9:3), and this overzealousness caused him to lead his people into bondage, "being deceived by the cunning and craftiness of king Laman" (Mosiah 7:21).

The experience of a man I will call Fred provides a more contemporary example of how restraint and anxious engagement might work in tandem, as complementary gifts. Inspired by the example of individuals like Brown-White, who donate their kidneys to strangers in need, Fred explored the possibility of donating his own kidney. He collected his urine so that doctors could verify the health of his kidneys and spent several weeks enduring a variety of physical and psychological examinations. But as the process for donation proceeded, Fred received a distinct impression through the Spirit, communicating something like the following: *You can choose to donate your kidney to save another's life. That is a worthy use of your body and your agency and would be pleasing to Me. But doing so will prevent you from accomplishing one or more of the missions for which I have prepared you.* When he recognized that donating a kidney would prevent him from pursuing important opportunities to serve others, Fred exercised restraint and focused his efforts elsewhere, volunteering at the local food bank and as a temple ordinance worker. Although these forms of service were less dramatic than Brown-White's donation of a kidney or Teancum's nighttime raids, Fred was no less anxiously engaged in good causes than these heroic figures.

Now, as in Teancum's day, the growth and progress of God's kingdom on earth depends upon the anxious engagement of its members, upon women and men who act without first receiving an assignment—without command or compulsion or a calling. Many of the programs that we now think of as central to the Church's mission began as the initiative of a single member who saw a need or a good cause and took it upon themselves to address that need. The Primary, Sunday School, Church Welfare Program, and Perpetual Education Fund were grassroots efforts adopted by the larger Church after the anxious engagement of a single member provided an efficacious model for accomplishing the work of salvation. As Elder Clayton M. Christensen attests, "We are urged at every level of the Church to question whether there is a better way of building the kingdom of God. The phrase, 'We believe that He will yet reveal many great and important things pertaining to the Kingdom of God' (Articles of Faith 1:9) does not have an expiration date on the package."[10] Whether or not our anxious engagement in good causes results in Church-wide change, we have each been charged with bringing to pass much righteousness. Our power to do so is innate, and every effort to develop this gift will be answered with divine aid in identifying which good causes deserve our attention and how we can best contribute to their accomplishment.

---

10 An aside note by Clayton M. Christensen in *The Power of Everyday Missionaries: The What and How of Sharing the Gospel* (Salt Lake City, UT: Deseret Book, 2012), 34.

CHAPTER 8
NEPHI, SON OF HELAMAN, AND THE GIFT OF UNWEARYINGNESS

LIVING IN A WORLD DEFINED by sin, political turmoil, domestic terrorism, and natural disasters, Nephi, the son of Helaman, wielded the power of God to work miracles. He sealed up the heavens so that there was no rain in the land for four years, causing a famine that persuaded the people to repent. He was "taken by the Spirit and conveyed" from place to place, traveling "in the Spirit, from multitude to multitude," so that he could share the gospel message more efficiently (Helaman 10:16–17). At the moment when a mob threatened to kill Nephi and his brother, Lehi, "a pillar of fire" descended to protect them, "and they were as standing in the midst of fire and were not burned" (Helaman 5:23–24). He received "many revelations daily," including, on one occasion, a revelation identifying the man who had assassinated the chief judge and providing step-by-step directions for securing evidence of the murder and proving his guilt (Helaman 11:23). Few figures in sacred history have exercised so many different spiritual gifts with such frequency and to such spectacular effect. And yet, the source of Nephi's power and his standing with God was a spiritual gift so modest and unassuming that some might hesitate to group it with the other, publicly visible gifts he possessed.

Before bestowing on Nephi the power "that whatsoever ye shall seal on earth shall be sealed in heaven; and whatsoever ye shall loose on earth shall be loosed in heaven," the Lord explained why He was entrusting such broad authority to a single man (Helaman 10:7). God declared that Nephi would be blessed because

> I have beheld how thou hast with unwearyingness declared the word, which I have given unto thee, unto this people. And thou hast not feared them, and hast not sought thine own life, but hast sought my will, and to keep my commandments.
>
> And now, because thou hast done this with such unwearyingness, behold, I will bless thee forever; and I will

> make thee mighty in word and in deed, in faith and in works; yea, even that all things shall be done unto thee according to thy word, for thou shalt not ask that which is contrary to my will. (Helaman 10:4–5)

Nephi's joyful diligence in sharing the gospel and in keeping the commandments persuaded the Lord that he could be trusted with the powers of heaven. His patient and persistent faithfulness in "a few things" led to a position of responsibility over "many things" (Matthew 25:21). Although many other spiritual gifts might seem more desirable, none is more necessary to our eternal progression, as we seek to imitate the Father and His Son, than the gift of unwearyingness.

Nephi's namesake, the son of Lehi, describes our progression along the covenant path and the need for unwearyingness in terms familiarized by the fourth Article of Faith. Faith and repentance must lead to baptism by immersion, for the remission of sins, and a second baptism of fire and of the Holy Ghost. Having outlined these requirements for salvation, Nephi, son of Lehi, asks "if all is done? Behold, I say unto you, Nay. . . . Wherefore, ye must press forward with a steadfastness in Christ, having a perfect brightness of hope, and a love of God and of all men. Wherefore, if ye shall press forward, feasting upon the word of Christ, and endure to the end, behold, thus saith the Father: Ye shall have eternal life" (2 Nephi 31:19–20). Eternal life, or "all that my Father hath," is promised not to those who simply enter upon the covenant path through baptism but to those who press forward steadfastly and endure to its end (D&C 84:38). Baptism, confirmation, and other ordinances are milestones along the covenant path; enduring to the end *is* the path. As the Lord declared to Enoch, "Endless and Eternal is my name" (Moses 7:35), and in our efforts to follow and become like our "Eternal Father," little is of more consequence than our willingness to develop an eternal—or unwearying—character through the cultivation of eternal, unceasing habits (D&C 20:77, 79). It is not enough, in our desire to learn divinity, that we demonstrate gratitude or gather others with love or anxiously engage in good works. Our gratitude and gathering and anxious engagement must be unwearying: felt and performed with the same good cheer on the thousandth or ten thousandth occasion that was manifest on the first.

Nephi, son of Helaman, was lauded for his unwearyingness in preaching the gospel, and the scriptural record attests to his persistent missionary efforts. Like his great-grandfather, Alma the Younger, he resigned from a prestigious career as chief judge of the Nephite nation to declare the word as a full-time missionary thirty years before the Savior's birth, devoting "all the remainder of his days" to teaching the gospel (Helaman 5:4). With his brother, Lehi, he taught "among all the people of Nephi, beginning at the city Bountiful; and from thenceforth to the city of Gid; and from the city of Gid to the city of Mulek; and even from one city to another, until they had gone forth among all the people of Nephi who were in the land southward; and from thence into the land of Zarahemla, among the Lamanites" (Helaman 5:14–16). To teach *all* the Nephites, visiting *every* city, would have been a lengthy, protracted endeavor, to which he then added a mission to the Lamanites. The fruits of his visit to the Lamanites were plentiful, such that "the Lamanites had become, the more part of them, a righteous people" (Helaman 6:1). Indeed, Nephi's preaching was so effective that the people he converted followed his example, "striving with unwearied diligence that they may bring the remainder of their brethren to the knowledge of the truth" (Helaman 15:6). In all, Nephi would seem to have spent thirty years of his life as a full-time missionary—"baptizing, and prophesying, and preaching, crying repentance unto the people, showing signs and wonders, working miracles among the people . . . telling them of things which must shortly come, that they might know and remember at the time of their coming that they had been made known unto them beforehand" (Helaman 16:4–5). Such a lengthy period of service suggests a consistent, unwavering commitment to living and sharing the gospel; he did not tire of declaring the word as his missionary labors extended across three decades.

The duration of Nephi's service is a good indication of his unwearyingness, but anyone who has served a full-time mission will attest that a period of protracted service may induce fatigue. The enduring intensity of our evangelical zeal is one key characteristic that distinguishes unwearyingness from the related but lesser gift of longsuffering. Surely Nephi, during his three decades of preaching, felt the same permanent enthusiasm that defined the ministry of Parley P. Pratt, perhaps the greatest missionary of this latter-day dispensation. Exhorting the elders of the Church to a greater diligence in their labors, Parley promised that their best efforts would be answered with the arrival of heavenly help, sustaining them in their labors. He declared,

> you will find that there is a spirit upon you which will urge you to continued exertion, and will never suffer you to feel at ease in Zion while a work remains unfinished in the great plan of redemption. . . . A spirit has been given you. And you will find, if you undertake to rest, it will be the hardest work you ever performed. I came home here from a foreign

mission. I presented myself to our President, and inquired what I should do next. "Rest," said he.

If I had been set to turn the world over, to dig down a mountain, to go to the ends of the earth, or traverse the deserts of Arabia, it would have been easier than to have undertaken to rest, while the Priesthood was upon me. I have received the holy anointing, and I can never rest till the last enemy is conquered, death destroyed, and truth reigns triumphant.[1]

Significantly, Parley does not claim that his feverish fervor for the work is inherent or a product of his own righteousness; rather, it is a gift available to all those who enlist in the army of God. He promises that those who seek to lose themselves in the service of God will receive the same heavenly aid that compelled Nephi to persist in the ministry despite occasional feelings of discouragement. The spiritual gift of unwearyingness is distinguished by the continuing enthusiasm or zeal with which we consistently engage in God's work.

The same zeal which characterized the preaching of Nephi and Parley similarly motivated the unceasing efforts of a stake Relief Society president in Brazil, Vilma Figuereda. Her ministry to the members in Campinas was defined by a spirit of great excitement. Elder James E. Faust wrote that after her conversion, President Figuereda was filled with "energy, conviction, and a desire to tell all of her acquaintances and others of the healing and sanctifying message of the gospel. She walked over so many cobblestones and on so many sidewalks that she would wear out a pair of shoes each month."[2] Her discarded shoes were an outward sign of her unwearyingness, but it was the energy and excitement motivating President Figuereda's continuous efforts that marked her service as an outgrowth of this spiritual gift. The pep in our step matters just as much as the total number of steps we take each day.

If the missionary service of Nephi, Parley, and President Figuereda seems daunting, we can take comfort in the fact that the gift of unwearyingness is most often manifest in our approach to the small and simple things of the gospel and not only in our outreach as member missionaries. Indeed, the very word *unwearyingness* should be a reminder of scriptural exhortations to "be not weary in well-doing, for ye are laying the foundation of a great work. And out of small things proceedeth that which is great" (D&C 64:33; see also 2 Thessalonians 3:13 and Galatians 6:9). Most members will not serve thirty-year missions or

---

1 Parley P. Pratt, "Spiritual Communication," in *Journal of Discourses*, 1:15.
2 James E. Faust, *To Reach Even Unto You* (Salt Lake City, UT: Deseret Book, 1980), 33.

wear out shoes on a monthly basis, but every follower of Jesus Christ is supposed to persevere in the simple duties that maintain our connection to heaven: prayer, scripture study, and church attendance, among others.[3] These are the "small things" from which the "great work" of our conversion comes into being, as we welcome the Savior into our lives. For some, merely finding time for scripture study, prayer, and the other "small things" of the gospel is a struggle; their spiritual foundations are laid painstakingly, one brick at a time, and they feel the full weight of every brick. But others are energized by these small things, and instead of falling asleep on their knees or while staring at their scriptures, they lose themselves in prayer and have to be torn away from their study of the Bible, Book of Mormon, Doctrine and Covenants, and Pearl of Great Price. They attend to these small and simple duties with the spiritual gift of unwearyingness.

Consider again the example of Nephi, son of Helaman, who prayed—as well as preached—with unwearyingness. Frustrated, at one point, by the Nephites' rejection of his message, Nephi approached the Lord in prayer to petition for his aid and express "the agony of his soul" (Helaman 7:6). This was not a routine morning prayer offered after Nephi rolled out of bed in the morning or a rote prayer of thanks offered before Nephi climbed into his bed at night; instead, this particular petition seems to have been offered during the middle of the day, "upon a tower, which was in the garden of Nephi, which was by the highway which led to the chief market" (Helaman 7:10). Nephi prayed so fervently that those traveling on the highway to market "saw Nephi as he was pouring out his soul unto God upon the tower; and they ran and told the people what they had seen, and the people came together in multitudes that they might know the cause of so great mourning for the wickedness of the people" (Helaman 7:11). Nephi's prayer was not a passive event; even from a distance, these observers could see the passion with which he offered his orisons to the Lord. Perhaps he rent his clothes or attired himself in ashes or beat his breast or wept. Whatever visible signs alerted passersby to the fervency of his mourning and prayer, these signs persisted long enough that by the time Nephi "arose" from his knees, a multitude had gathered (Helaman 7:12). The timing, intensity, and duration of Nephi's prayer suggest that he prayed unceasingly and with an attitude of unwearyingness.

Our own prayers need not be accompanied with gestures that would cause alarm or draw a crowd, but most of us would do well to increase the frequency, intensity, and duration of our private, personal petitions to the Lord so that we, too, might be said to pray with unwearyingness. President Sydney S. Reynolds

---

3 See Dallin H. Oaks, "Small and Simple Things," *Ensign* or *Liahona*, May 2018.

of the Primary General Presidency reminds us that we can pray "in many places. I have prayed on the beach, in the mountains, in church, on the playground. I have prayed in my house, in an airplane, and at the hospital."[4] A bishop of my acquaintance developed a habit facilitating this flexible approach to prayer. Each morning when he dressed, he would place a pencil and small, lined slips of paper in his pocket so that whenever the Holy Ghost brought the needs of a ward member to his memory, he could write down his or her name. This small act of remembrance was, in itself, a form of prayer, as he offered a silent petition to the Lord whenever he recorded their names. Later, when he made his way to the temple, those small slips of paper would be placed on the prayer roll; this habit expanded his capacity for the effort-intensive, System 2 thinking described in chapter one. Individuals like this bishop and President Reynolds pray so frequently because they feel comfort, joy, and confidence in conversing with the Father in the name of Jesus Christ; it is this attitude, even more than the total number or length of their prayers, that distinguishes their supplications.

Similarly, it is an attitude and not the total number of hours or pages read that distinguishes an unwearying study of the scriptures from forced marches through the standard works. Seminary students, missionaries, and others may read regularly for the wrong reasons. As a result, their time in the scriptures may feel like a burden rather than a blessing. To read with unwearyingness is to experience the joy and spiritual hunger described by Parley in his first encounter with the Book of Mormon: "I commenced its contents by course. I read all day; eating was a burden, I had no desire for food; sleep was a burden when the night came, for I preferred reading to sleep."[5] Preoccupied with the spiritual feast offered in the Book of Mormon, Pratt experienced a feeling of energized focus and deep immersion in the scriptures, such that he could study for a far longer period without attending to basic needs of the flesh than would normally have been possible, a feeling that Mormon characterizes as being "swallowed up in the joy of Christ." When Alma and his companions preached to the Zoramites, "the Lord provided for them that they should hunger not, neither should they thirst; yea, and he also gave them strength, that they should suffer no manner of afflictions, save it were swallowed up in the joy of Christ" (Alma 31:38). One interpretation of this verse is that Alma, Ammon, Aaron, Omner, Amulek, and Zeezrom were so

---

[4] Shirley S. Reynolds, "I Can Pray to Heavenly Father Anytime, Anywhere," *Ensign* or *Liahona*, May 2003.

[5] Parley P. Pratt, *The Autobiography of Parley Parker Pratt* (New York: Russell Brothers, 1874), 38.

eager to share the gospel that, like Parley, they literally lost the desire to eat. As we apply and share gospel principles with unwearyingness, swallowed up in the joy of Christ, our priorities necessarily shift, and even physical imperatives such as sleeping and eating become less important.

Parley's joyful experience of reading the Book of Mormon might seem to establish an unrealistic standard for our daily scripture study. After all, he was reading for the first time, while many members of the Church are very familiar with the language and stories of sacred writ. But the immersive experience of being swallowed up in the scriptures is still available to those who read and seek with real intent. When a Relief Society sister I will call Rachael was asked what she was passionate about, she responded:

> Scriptures. Obsessed. It's the first thing I do in the morning and the last thing I do at night. . . . [While praying a few months ago] I was immediately overcome with this awesome desire to read the Book of Mormon. I stayed up until 4AM reading, and I continued binging until I finished a little less than a week later. I read with a completely open heart, which I intentionally kept open. My child-like adoration is apparent if you ever take a look at my Book of Mormon; it's quite colorful and full of pink hearts and doodles, covered in notes, thoughts, love. I call it, "My Book." My family knows what book I'm looking for if I ask where My Book is. I've re-read sections of it over and over again during the past few months. . . . It's not uncommon for me to lock the bathroom door and sit on the floor to read. It's what I want to do. . . . I feel pure comfort when I read the scriptures. My life and my family are so much better now. The blessings of feasting on God's word have trickled down into every part of my life and even pushed out the bad![6]

For Rachael, as for Parley, sleeping, eating, and other necessities of life have become distractions from scripture study rather than the activities she most anticipates. Hiding in the bathroom so that she can sneak in a few more verses, Rachael has come to truly love the scriptures and to search them with unwearyingness. She has learned for herself the truth of Elder Richard G. Scott's counsel that "feasting on the word of God each day is more important than sleep, school,

---

6 Personal correspondence in possession of the author.

work, television shows, video games, or social media."⁷ When our care for the creature and other matters of this world become distractions, rather than our main concerns, we will have learned a measure of that unwearyingness that is necessary to complete our eternal journey.

Learning to pray or to study the scriptures or to preach the gospel with unwearyingness is primarily a matter of schooling our desires on a daily, hourly, and even minute-by-minute basis.⁸ For this reason, one of the appointed means by which we might come to receive this spiritual gift is through obedience to the Lord's law of health. From birth, our physical bodies are filled with desires, particularly for food, drink, and sleep. But a loving Heavenly Father revealed to Joseph Smith a need to regulate these impulses so that we eat and drink and rest with moderation. To those who obey His law of health, which has been adapted "to the capacity of the weak and the weakest of all saints, who are or can be called saints," God promises the blessing of unwearyingness (D&C 89:3). He invites us to "cease to sleep longer than is needful; retire to thy bed early, that ye may not be weary; arise early, that your bodies and your minds may be invigorated" (D&C 88:124). These commands are, perhaps, more difficult to keep today than ever before. We live at a time when artificial light is cheap and abundant, when entertainment options multiply at a dizzying pace, and when it is possible for many to put food on the table without rising at dawn to milk the cows, gather the eggs, or harvest the grain that they will eat. It is easy to lose ourselves in the latest movie or video game and stay up later than we should, only to sleep in later than we should. But to those who will school their desires for late-night entertainment and resist temptations to snooze the morning away, God promises energy and insight: bodies and minds that respond to the demands of each new day with unwearyingness.

A comparable promise is made to all who temper their appetite for food and drink. The Word of Wisdom warns against the ingestion of addictive compounds, such as those found in alcohol, tobacco, and hot drinks, such as tea or coffee; consuming these and other addictive substances progressively limits both our range of choices and our ability to choose, replacing moral agency with bodily desire as the governing principle in our lives. But the Lord also prescribes moderation in the consumption of food and drink which He "hath ordained for the constitution, nature, and use of man—every herb in the season thereof, and every fruit in the season thereof; all these to be used with prudence and

---

7 Richard G. Scott, "Make the Exercise of Faith Your First Priority," *Ensign* or *Liahona*, Nov. 2014.
8 See Dallin H. Oaks, "Desire," *Ensign* or *Liahona*, May 2011.

thanksgiving" (D&C 89:10–11). Prudence is the ability to discipline desire and govern ourselves with wisdom; our appetites are to be educated and constrained, such that we consume that which is in season and eat meat, as well as other delicacies, "sparingly" (D&C 89:12). To those who school their cravings for food and drink, the Lord promises marvelous blessings: "all saints who remember to keep and do these sayings, walking in obedience to the commandments, shall receive health in their navel and marrow to their bones; and shall find wisdom and great treasures of knowledge, even hidden treasures; and shall run and not be weary, and shall walk and not faint" (D&C 89:18–20). These promises of physical stamina and mental acuity enlarge upon the assurances made to those who retire early in the evening and arise early in the morning. Obeying the Lord's law of health requires consistent and continuous efforts, but the blessings accompanying such efforts increase our capacity to act "with all the energy of heart" required (Moroni 7:48). Those who seek the spiritual gift of unwearyingness should begin their efforts to develop this aptitude by keeping the Word of Wisdom more exactly.

This link between a love for the Word of Wisdom and the spiritual gift of unwearyingness is plainly evident in the life and ministry of President Heber J. Grant, seventh prophet of the Restoration. During his apostolic ministry, Elder Grant railed against the evils of alcohol, tobacco, coffee, and tea with such fervor and frequency that in 1909, one of his senior Brethren felt it necessary to direct that he speak about something else. Elder Grant wrote in his journal that "a great many people had remarked to him that they were getting somewhat tired of my constantly preaching upon this subject, and he would like to have me talk on the peaceable things of the kingdom" instead.[9] This intervention resulted in a two-year cease-fire, after which Elder Grant returned to his favorite topic with full-throated enthusiasm. Throughout the nineteenth and early twentieth centuries, members—and even some leaders—of the Church felt themselves at liberty to disregard the counsel offered in the Word of Wisdom, treating the revelation as an admonition rather than a commandment. But through the pervasive message of President Grant, his "repetitious sermons" and "constant preachments, cajoling and exhorting the members to observe the Word of Wisdom," this law of health became a core, identifying doctrine of the Latter-day Saint faith.[10] His tireless, unceasing message to the Saints throughout an apostolic ministry of more than sixty years was, eventually, internalized by the membership of the Church.

---

9 Francis M. Gibbons, *Heber J. Grant: Man of Steel, Prophet of God* (Salt Lake City, UT: Deseret Book, 1979), 155.

10 Gibbons, *Heber J. Grant*, 158.

President Grant loved the Word of Wisdom and taught the doctrine with unwearyingness, but this spiritual gift was also manifest in his private life, as he cultivated talents and pursued goals with a persistent and joyful diligence that has become legendary. Stories illustrating his unrelenting and unwavering perseverance abound. As a youth, Grant was mocked by peers for his poor penmanship; he responded by vowing that one day he would write better than their teacher—and, in time, he did. His hand improved so much that he eventually earned a significant income by penning the script for holiday greeting cards. His development as a baseball player followed a similar trajectory. After being mocked for his inability to throw with force and accuracy, being relegated to a junior team with players several years younger than him, Grant vowed that he would one day play on the team that won the Utah territorial championship—and after hours and hours of practice, during which the sound of his baseball thumping against the bishop's barn became a metronome for the neighborhood, he did. His development as a singer was similarly owing to his unwearyingness. Tone deaf, he enlisted the help of a music teacher. After two hours of practice, President Grant recounted, "I still couldn't sing one line from the song we had been practicing. After practicing that one song for more than five thousand times, I made a mess of it when I tried to sing it in public. I practiced it for another six months. Now I can learn a song in a few hours."[11] Diligence and perseverance allowed President Grant to overcome weaknesses and physical limitations.

In like manner, the gift of unwearyingness is essential in our efforts to overcome sin and "the weakness which is in [us], according to the flesh" (1 Nephi 19:6). Our moral failings and other weaknesses are made strong through Jesus Christ, but He requires "the heart and a willing mind" before He will work in our lives (D&C 64:34; see also Ether 12:27 and Philippians 4:13). In other words, His capacity to lift and strengthen and bless us is predicated on our desires; only when we desire righteousness with unwearyingness can we receive the strength and power granted to Nephi, son of Helaman. If such a standard seems daunting, we can take courage in the teachings of Alma, who reminds us that our best efforts are always magnified and multiplied. Thus, he instructs those who "can no more than desire" to "let this desire work in you" until it grows and leads us to more and more consistent efforts (Alma 32:27). Small and simple efforts to live the Word of Wisdom or to offer heartfelt prayers or to study the scriptures can crescendo into an unwearying commitment to live these gospel principles. The promises that Alma offers, with respect to scripture study, apply to other pursuits in our lives:

11 *Teachings of Presidents of the Church: Heber J. Grant* [2002], 35.

> If ye will nourish the word, yea, nourish the tree as it beginneth to grow, by your faith with great diligence, and with patience, looking forward to the fruit thereof, it shall take root; and behold it shall be a tree springing up unto everlasting life.
>
> And because of your diligence and your faith and your patience with the word in nourishing it, that it may take root in you, behold, by and by ye shall pluck the fruit thereof, which is most precious, which is sweet above all that is sweet, and which is white above all that is white, yea, and pure above all that is pure; and ye shall feast upon this fruit even until ye are filled, that ye hunger not, neither shall ye thirst.
>
> Then, my brethren, ye shall reap the rewards of your faith, and your diligence, and patience, and long-suffering, waiting for the tree to bring forth fruit unto you. (Alma 32:41–43)

The fruit of eternal life can come only through diligence and patience and joyful perseverance—through unwearyingness.

As we school our desires, we learn to persist in small and simple things, until we, like Nephi, can be entrusted with the great work of God. "That 'great work,'" Elder Jeffrey R. Holland once taught, "is what, with effort and patience and God's help, you can become."[12] Our becoming is necessarily a long and drawn-out process: hence the need for unwearyingness. No one with a true appreciation for the majesty and power and mercy of God can possibly suppose that he or she is a brief interlude or one concerted effort away from perfection. We will, along the way, encounter opposition and pains and frustration and sorrows, just as Nephi did. Simply enduring these trials and persisting is not enough; if we would receive "the riches of eternity," we must endure them well and "be of good cheer" in our diligent embrace of hard work, strenuous effort, and prolonged struggle (D&C 78:18). Finding strength to go forward with gladness is the essence of unwearyingness, and those who desire to receive all that the Father has must first seek for and receive this precious spiritual gift. Only then, when we have learned to persist in well-doing with unwearyingness, without regard for discomfort or discouragement, will we be able to answer the charge given us by the prophet Joseph Smith: "Brethren, shall we not go on in so great a cause? Go forward and not backward. Courage, brethren; and on, on to the victory! Let your hearts rejoice, and be exceedingly glad" (D&C 128:22).

---

12 Jeffrey R. and Patricia T. Holland, "However Long and Hard the Road" [Brigham Young University devotional, Jan. 18, 1983], speeches.byu.edu.

AFTERWORD
A MORE EXCELLENT WAY

IN HIS FIRST EPISTLE TO the Corinthians, the Apostle Paul offered both a caution and an exhortation at the conclusion of his writings on spiritual gifts. He taught, in summation, "covet earnestly the best gifts: and yet shew I unto you a more excellent way" (1 Corinthians 12:31). Moroni elaborated upon that theme, declaring that "in the gift of his Son hath God prepared a more excellent way" (Ether 12:11). The "best gifts" described in this book are not, in themselves, an end, and anyone who seeks spiritual gifts for fame or for personal gain has forgotten the nature and purpose of these gifts, which come from and through Christ—*the* Gift—in order to turn our hearts more fully to Him. Unless our earnest seeking for spiritual gifts results in a more charitable and Christ-like life, that seeking is in vain. Like other prophets before and after him, Elder James E. Faust warned against the spiritually immature practice of seeking for signs in spiritual gifts and treating their manifestations as cause for titillation: "Rather than being like a drug, the gifts of the spirit that true religion brings work differently. They do not excite; they calm. They do not hallucinate; they strengthen. They do not weaken; they make more powerful. They are not mere escape hatches from responsibilities, but instruments of insight into what life really means."[1] The purpose and meaning of our lives is clear: we are to find joy (see 2 Nephi 2:25) through the accomplishment of our "work, to keep [the] commandments" (D&C 11:20), so that the Father and Son may accomplish their work—"the immortality and eternal life of man" (Moses 1:39).[2] Spiritual gifts are worth remembering and pursuing only insofar as they turn our hearts more firmly toward the merits and mercies of Jesus Christ. Moving forward in that more excellent way, and helping others to do the same, is the only purpose for which we can appropriately seek these best-of-all gifts.

---

1 James E. Faust, *To Reach Even unto You* (Salt Lake City, UT: Deseret Book, 1980), 120–21.
2 See David A. Bednar, "The Tender Mercies of the Lord," *Ensign* or *Liahona*, May 2005.

To that end, reviewing the consecrated life of President Thomas S. Monson is instructive. At President Monson's death, Elder Jeffrey R. Holland said that our sixteenth prophet "had a special gift for personal, one-on-one ministration that he honed throughout his life. . . . [He] was an example of someone who refined and magnified a spiritual gift. . . . 'We either identify with being the recipient of such a gift,' Elder Holland said, 'or we might hope and dream that some day we might be good enough to do that ourselves.'"[3] The stories of President Monson's personal ministry to the one are numerous and inspiring. His care for each of the many widows in his ward lasted long after he had been released from serving as their bishop. His visits to hospitals, nursing homes, and bedsides allowed him to offer priesthood blessings of comfort and healing at precisely the moment they were needed. Because of his unwearying efforts to magnify the spiritual gifts he had been given, President Monson was able to help thousands and tens of thousands to progress along the more excellent way established by Jesus Christ. To paraphrase a popular Primary song—in our desires to receive and magnify spiritual gifts, as in all else, we should follow the prophet; he knows the more excellent way.

The lives of President Monson and other prophets, both ancient and modern, serve as guideposts along that more excellent way. They are those described in scripture, to whom "it may be given to have all those gifts, that there may be a head, in order that every member may be profited thereby" (D&C 46:29). Faithful attention to the words and deeds of the prophets will result in an increased understanding of the spiritual gifts they possess, enabling disciples to receive a greater portion of those gifts for themselves and draw closer to the Savior. Elder Neil L. Andersen has shown us this pattern in the life of President Russell M. Nelson:

> In 1982, two years before being called as a General Authority, Brother Russell M. Nelson said: "I never ask myself, 'When does the prophet speak as a prophet and when does he not?' My interest has been, 'How can I be more like him?' And he added, 'My [philosophy is to] stop putting question marks behind the prophet's statements and put exclamation points instead.'" This is how a humble and spiritual man chose to order his life. Now, 36 years later, he is the Lord's prophet.[4]

---

3 As quoted in Tad Walch, "President Thomas S. Monson, 16th Prophet of the LDS Church, Dies After a Lifetime Spent Going 'to the Rescue,'" *Deseret News*, January 2, 2018, https://www.deseretnews.com/article/900006756A/president-thomas-s-monson-16th-prophet-of-the-lds-church-dies-after-a-lifetime-spent-going-to-the-rescue.html.

4 Neil L. Andersen, "The Prophet of God," *Ensign* or *Liahona*, May 2018.

As Brother Nelson gave humble heed to the teachings of Presidents Spencer W. Kimball, Ezra Taft Benson, Howard W. Hunter, Gordon B. Hinckley, Thomas S. Monson, and their predecessors, he qualified to receive a greater portion of the gifts available to God's children, until he, too, was made "a head" of the Church. Obviously, not all who follow his example can be ordained to the apostleship—but all who do so can and will grow "from grace to grace," from gift to gift, until they, too, receive a fullness (D&C 93:13).

This outpouring of spiritual power and gifts has been promised to every Latter-day Saint who follows the example of the prophets and works to build up the kingdom of God. When Nephi saw our times in vision, the Lord declared: "blessed are they who shall seek to bring forth my Zion at that day, for they shall have the gift and the power of the Holy Ghost" (1 Nephi 13:37). The constant companionship of the Holy Ghost is only one of the many precious gifts made available to the men, women, and children of this dispensation. The Lord is eager to open the windows of heaven and pour out blessings upon the heads of His people, but these blessings "are made conditional on our asking for them. Blessings require some work or effort on our part before we can obtain them" (Bible Dictionary, "Prayer"). Those willing to undertake this work can take comfort in the sure promise given by Jesus Christ to His ancient disciples, which still applies to our own day and to our own righteous desires for spiritual gifts: "Ask, and it shall be given you; seek, and ye shall find; knock, and it shall be opened unto you" (Matthew 7:7). Each who "asketh in Spirit shall receive in Spirit" because "he that asketh in the Spirit asketh according to the will of God; wherefore it is done even as he asketh" (D&C 46:28, 30). As our desires are brought into alignment with the will of God and we persevere in the work required to realize those desires, we will qualify for all the blessings a loving Father desires to bestow upon us—including His best gifts.

ABOUT THE AUTHOR

Zachary McLeod Hutchins is an associate professor of English at Colorado State University, where he writes and teaches about early American literature and religious culture. The lucky husband of Alana Esther Hutchins, he is a father to seven very rambunctious children, who are growing up far too fast. He hopes, someday, to be called as a Nursery leader, so he can get back to playing with toddlers and eating snacks during church.